Make IT Now — Bake IT Later!

All "Make-Aheads" — Fun, easy, and Tasty!

Combines all six smaller books!

by Barbara Goodfellow

A Fireside Book Published by Simon & Schuster New

Revised Fireside Edition, 1982
Published by Simon & Schuster, Inc.
Simon & Schuster Building
Rockefeller Center
1230 Avenue of the Americas
New York, New York 10020

FIRESIDE and colophon are registered trademarks of
Simon & Schuster, Inc.

Manufactured in the United States of America

10 9 8 7 6 5 4 3 2 Pbk.

Library of Congress Cataloging in Publication Data

Goodfellow, Barbara
Make it Now — Bake it Later!
"A Fireside Book"
    Includes index
    1. Cookery 1. Title
TX715. G6518 1982 641.5'55 82-730
ISBN 0-671-45082-4 Pbk. AACR2

This "Complete Make It Now — Bake It Later!" is dedicated To The memory of

Courtenay Pickett McLaughlin
a brave young girl —
a valiant struggle —
and all along The way she
brightened The days for others.

Each page of This book brings my real Thanks To my dear family and The many generous friends who, Throughout more Than Twenty years, have helped me To make This project a success.

Contents

Cont'd

Party Chicken

A new combination but still so easy!

8 good sized chicken breasts
   Ask your meat man to skin and
   bone them.
8 slices bacon
1 pkg. chipped beef - about 4 oz.
1 can undiluted mushroom soup
½ pint commercial sour cream

Wrap each chicken breast with a
   piece of bacon.
Cover bottom of flat greased baking
   dish (about 8" x 12" x 2") with
   chipped beef.
Arrange chicken breasts on chipped
   beef.
Mix soup and sour cream and pour over
   all. Refrigerate.
When ready, bake at 275° for 3 hours,
   uncovered.

Serves 8 —

1

You'll Never Believe It!

This can be started in mid-afternoon
but don't ask me why it works —

Any size rib roast of beef
Salt and pepper — no flour

Place beef in roasting pan, uncovered,
    and put in 375° oven for 1 hour.
Turn off the oven, but do <u>not</u> open
    the oven door at all.

For rare roast beef:
    45 minutes before serving time
    turn oven to 300°.

For medium roast beef:
    50 minutes before serving time
    turn oven to 300°.

For medium well done roast beef:
    55 minutes before serving time
    turn oven to 300°.

That's all — don't peek!

2

Cheesy Zucchini Bake

It's Tasty, easy, lo-cal, and inexpensive!
What more can you ask?

- 1 lb. lean ground beef
- ½ yellow onion, chopped
- ½ Teaspoon garlic powder
- 1 lb. fresh zucchini
- 6 oz. (generous) longhorn cheese, freshly grated
- 1 can (10¾ oz.) mushroom soup, undiluted

Brown meat with onion and garlic powder. Drain off any excess grease.

Wash zucchini and cut off Tips. Do not peel. Cut in ¼" slices. Cook for no more Than 5 minutes in small amount of boiling water. Drain.

Grease a 1½ QT. baking dish and put in a layer of half The meat - Then half The zucchini - Then half The cheese. Repeat layers.

Mix soup with ¼ cup water and pour over Top.

Refrigerate. When ready, bake at 350° for 40 minutes, uncovered.

(I Tried it with regular cheddar. Good, but not nearly as good as with longhorn!)

Serves 4 - maybe!

3

Party Salad for Ten

To me, this recipe alone is worth
the cost of the book!

½ pkg. (10 oz. pkg.) fresh spinach, torn in pieces
   salt and pepper to taste — ½ teaspoon sugar
6 hardboiled eggs, finely chopped
½ lb. julienne boiled ham (I use the cello pkgs.
   of sandwich ham and slice thin)
1 small or ½ large head iceberg lettuce, torn
   or shredded
   salt and pepper to taste — ½ teaspoon sugar
1 pkg. (10 oz.) frozen peas, thawed but not
   cooked
1 red Bermuda onion, peeled and thinly
   sliced
1 cup commercial sour cream
1 pint real mayonnaise
½ lb. julienne Swiss cheese
½ lb. bacon, crisply cooked and crumbled

It is important to drain everything well.

In the bottom of a large glass or wooden
   salad bowl, spread the spinach.
   Sprinkle with salt, pepper and sugar.
Add a layer of the eggs.

        cont'd

Party Salad for Ten (cont'd.)

Add a layer of the ham.

Add a layer of lettuce and sprinkle with salt, pepper and sugar.

Scatter peas over all.

Pull onion slices into rings and spread on salad.

Mix sour cream and mayonnaise and spread evenly all over top.

Arrange cheese over all.

Cover bowl with plastic wrap and refrigerate overnight.

Just before serving, sprinkle with bacon.

Do <u>not</u> toss. Serve portions all the way to the bottom of the bowl.

For a main course salad meal, you can substitute tuna, crab, shrimp or lobster for the bacon.

Saucy Pork Chops

My husband's favorite recipe for pork!

1/2 cup ketchup
1 1/2 Teaspoons salt
1/2 Teaspoon chili powder
1 cup water
1/2 Tablespoon dry mustard
1 Tablespoon brown sugar
4 loin pork chops (center cut-1 1/2" Thick)
1 lemon
1 yellow onion

Mix first 6 ingredients Together.
Put chops in flat greased baking
      dish — in one layer.
Pour sauce over chops.
Slice lemon and onion and arrange
      one slice of each on each chop.
Refrigerate.
When ready To bake, place in 325°
      oven, covered, for 2 hours.
Remove cover and baste well with
      The sauce.
Continue baking, uncovered, for
      1/2 hour more.
Spoon sauce over chops again
      before serving.

Serves 4

6

Dinner in a Packet

Particularly for the Teenage cooks!

Ingredients per person:
- 1 shoulder or round bone lamb chop
- 1 slice green pepper
- 1 slice yellow onion
- 1 carrot — a thick one
- 1/4 pkg. mushroom gravy mix (about 1 oz. pkg.) dry!
- 1 slice Tomato — Thick

Grease a large piece of foil (about 14")
Put chop in center of foil.
On Top of chop put green pepper.
Then put onion on top of pepper.
Peel carrot and slice lengthwise into 4 slices. Arrange around chop.
Sprinkle gravy mix over all.
Top with Tomato.
Refrigerate in foil packet.
    To make packet bring edges of foil Together and seal with a double fold.
When ready To bake, place on rack in 350° oven for 1 hour.

7

London Chicken

So simple - and so delicious!

24 pieces of chicken (breasts, legs, and second joints)
    butter (enough to brown chicken)
¾ lb. sliced mushrooms (can use canned, drained)
2 cans cream of chicken soup
1 can mushroom soup
    sherry or white wine to taste - (about ¼ cup)

Brown the chicken in butter. Then brown mushrooms if using fresh ones.

Place chicken in a large casserole.

Mix the soups (undiluted) and pour over chicken.

Place mushrooms on top.

Refrigerate.

When ready to bake, add wine, cover the casserole, and bake at 350° for 1½ hours.

Serves 12

8

Lazyman's Stew

The meat browns nicely, and the gravy thickens. Wonderful flavour!

2 lbs. chuck stewmeat
1 pkg. dehydrated onion soup (1½ oz.)
1 can mushroom soup, undiluted
1 can (8 oz.) sliced mushrooms
     with juice

Mix all together and put in
     casserole.
Bake 3 hours at 325°, covered.

Serve with noodles or fluffy
     white rice.

Serves 4-6

9

Divine Tamale Pie

Everyone loves it!

Bottom layer:

    1/2 cup yellow corn meal
    1/2 teaspoon salt
    1 cup boiling water
    1 1/2 cups milk

Stir cornmeal and salt into boiling water in top of double boiler but over open flame. Stir until it is thickening – add milk – stir gently – and place over hot water. Simmer, covered, for 30 minutes. Line bottom of a well greased flat baking dish (2 qt. or 7 1/2" x 12") with this mush. Cool.

Filling:

    1 yellow onion sautéed in a little bacon grease
    1 1/2 lbs ground beef shoulder
    2 Tablespoons chili powder
    1 can cream style corn
    1 large can solid pack tomatoes
    salt to taste
    ripe pitted olives, whole

Sauté onion and remove from pan. Cook meat in the bacon fat (left from sautéeing the onion) until all red color is gone. Mix in the onion. Sprinkle chili powder over meat mixture and blend thoroughly. Add the corn and tomatoes, including the juice, but be sure to leave fairly large pieces of tomato

cont'd

10

Prairie Tamale Pie (Cont'd)

Throughout the filling.
Spoon this filling carefully on top
of the corn meal layer which is
firm and cool in the baking dish.
Salt and dot with ripe pitted olives.
Refrigerate.

Topping:
Just before baking, make Corn
Muffin Mix according to directions,
using one regular size or two
small packages.

Bake the Tamale Pie at 375° for
about 20 minutes or until top is
done. Then turn the oven low
for about 40 minutes longer so
it can cook slowly.

Remember to start this the day
ahead. The meat mixture has
more flavor if it stands.

Serves 6 amply —

Easy Chicken Casserole

"Easy" is right!

1 cup uncooked rice
1 can mushroom soup
1 pkg. dehydrated onion soup
1 1/2 soup cans of milk
1 large fryer, cut in serving pieces
    salt and pepper

Mix together the rice, soups, and
    milk. Place in a large casserole.
    (I use a 3 qt. size)
Put the chicken on top, skin side
    down and add salt and pepper
    to taste.

Make this 3 hours ahead of time.
    Place it in a 250° oven, uncovered,
    for 3 hours. Turn the chicken
    over once. That's all!

Serves 4

12

Crab and Shrimp

Fit for an embassy buffet!

1 1/2 pounds crabmeat
1/2 pound small shrimp
1/2 green pepper, chopped
1/3 cup parsley, chopped
2 cups cooked rice
1 1/2 cups real mayonnaise
2 packages frozen peas, thawed
   but not cooked
salt and pepper to taste

Toss lightly. Place in greased casserole. Refrigerate, covered.

Bake 1 hour at 350°, covered.

Serves 6

13

Lamb Shanks Deluxe

And so fragrant while baking!

4 meaty lamb shanks
1/2 lemon
1/4 Tsp. garlic powder - or more
1 cup all-purpose flour
2 Tsp. salt
1/2 Tsp. pepper
1/2 cup salad oil
1 can (10 1/2 oz.) condensed beef con-
    sommé, undiluted
1 cup water
1/2 cup dry vermouth
1 medium yellow onion, chopped
4 carrots, peeled and sliced in chunks
4 stalks celery, sliced in chunks

Rub lamb with lemon and sprinkle
    with garlic powder. Let stand 10
    minutes.
Combine flour, salt, and pepper in a
    paper bag. Shake shanks one at a
    time in bag to coat with flour.
    Save flour.
Brown shanks in hot oil in large,
    heavy skillet. Remove meat from
    pan. (cont'd.)   14

Lamb Shanks Deluxe (Cont'd)

Add 4 Tblsp. of the seasoned flour
to pan drippings and, using a
wire whip, stir and brown the
flour.

Add consommé, water, and vermouth,
and stir and cook until slightly
thickened. Add onion.

Place shanks in large baking dish
and pour over them the consommé
mixture. Shanks should be in
one layer only. Refrigerate.

When ready to bake, place in 300°
oven, uncovered, for 1½ hours.

Turn shanks, add carrots and celery,
and continue to bake one
more hour.

Gravy delicious over mashed potatoes.

Serves 4 —

15

Layers

Meat, potato, and vegetables all in one!

1 lb. lean ground beef
3 carrots, peeled and sliced
3 stalks celery, sliced
1 large baking potato, peeled and sliced
1 medium yellow onion, peeled and sliced
1 small green pepper - remove seeds and
    white membrane. Chop the pepper.
1 can (4 oz.) mushrooms, drained
salt and pepper to taste
1 teaspoon each dried basil and parsley
1/4 teaspoon dried tarragon
1 can (10 1/2 oz.) tomato soup, undiluted

Break up meat into bottom of 2 qt.
    baking dish.
Put carrots on top of meat, then celery,
    then potato slices, onion, green
    pepper and lastly, the mushrooms.
Add seasonings over all, and cover
    with tomato soup.
Refrigerate, covered.
When ready, place in 350° oven for
    2 hours, covered.

Good with green salad and hot
    French bread!

Serves 4 (if you want more, use 2
    large potatoes.)

16

No Work Chicken

So good — and it's best when prepared
the day before!

Chicken breasts for 4
½ cup honey
½ cup Dijon style wet mustard
1 Tablespoon curry powder
2 Tablespoons soy sauce

Place chicken snugly, skin side down, in
    flat baking dish in one layer
Make marinade by mixing together the
    honey, mustard, curry powder and
    soy sauce. Pour over chicken and
    refrigerate 6 hours or overnight.
When ready, turn chicken, cover dish
    with foil and bake at 350° for
    one hour. Remove foil — baste
    well — and continue baking,
    uncovered, for 15 more minutes.
When serving, spoon sauce over
    chicken.

Serves 4 —

17

Savory Sausage Casserole

Inexpensive and Tasty!

1 lb. bulk pork sausage (a good brand
    not too salty!)
1 cup uncooked rice
2 pkgs. (2 oz. each) dehydrated chicken
    noodle soup
1/4 cup finely chopped onion
1 cup sliced celery
2 1/2 cups water
1 Tblsp. soy sauce
1/2 cup toasted halved or slivered blanched
    almonds

Break apart the sausage and brown it in
    an ungreased skillet, pouring off any
    excess fat as it accumulates. Remove
    from the burner.

Mix together the sausage, rice, soup,
    onion, and celery and place in a
    2 qt. casserole.

Refrigerate.

When ready to bake, mix soy sauce with
    water and add this, with the almonds,
    to the casserole. Mix all gently.

Cover and bake at 350° for 1 hour.

Serves 6

18

Spanish Bean Pot

A delicious new version of an old
    favorite.

2 large (# 2½) cans red kidney beans
3 slices bacon
1 yellow onion
½ cup juice from can of peach halves
2 Tblsp. cider vinegar
¼ cup strong coffee

Drain beans, saving liquid.
Fry bacon and cut in small pieces.
Slice onion and fry in bacon grease.

Combine the above.

Then combine the following:
    1 clove garlic, grated
    1 pinch thyme
    1 pinch rosemary
    1 Tsp. salt
    1 bay leaf, broken
    2 Tsp. dry mustard
    ¼ Tsp. ground cloves
    ¼ Tsp. cayenne

Combine this second mixture
    with the first.   (contd)

Spanish Bean Pot (cont'd)

Place in greased casserole and refrigerate.

When ready to bake, place in very
slow oven 1 to 1½ hours.
Put 4 slices bacon on top the last
½ hour.
If it becomes too dry, add some
bean liquor.
Just before serving, add 1 jigger
brandy and stir casserole up
from the bottom to mix.

This can be made a day ahead,
baked when ready.

Peaches can be served as a side
dish with the beans.

If you double the recipe, do not
fully double the fruit juice
unless you want beans to
be very juicy!

Serves 6
(Refrigerate if made ahead —)

20

Dinner in a Dish

The family will like This!

1 chuck roast, about 3½ lbs.
   (preferably boneless and at least 2 inches Thick)
1 can cream of celery soup, undiluted
½ pkg. (1½ oz. pkg.) dehydrated onion soup
4 potatoes, peeled
4 carrots, peeled
8 celery stalks
¼ lb. fresh mushrooms
½ cup red wine

Place roast in bottom of large casserole
   or baking pan.
Spread celery soup on Top and sprinkle
   onion soup over all.
Cut potatoes in half and cut carrots in
   3-inch chunks. Add both.
Cover and bake at 350° for 1 hour.
Cut celery in 1-inch chunks and add,
   with mushrooms.
Add wine and spoon sauce up well over
   all The vegetables.
Continue baking, covered, for 1 hour more.

If you Transfer all This To a platter for
   serving, be sure To serve sauce from
   a gravy boat. It is so good on the
   potatoes.

Serves 6

21

Frozen Luncheon Sandwiches

A very popular recipe — and all you do
is bake them!

20 slices white sandwich bread
1½ cups diced cooked chicken
1 can (10½ oz.) mushroom soup, undiluted
½ can (10½ oz.) chicken gravy
2 Tablespoons drained, minced pimento
1 Tablespoon minced green onion
1 can (5 oz.) waterchestnuts, chopped
   salt to taste
8 eggs
4 Tablespoons milk
   Large bag potato chips, crushed
   Parsley

Trim crusts from bread.

Mix together the chicken, soup,
   gravy, pimento, onion and
   waterchestnuts. Add salt and
   mix well.

Divide this mixture equally among 10
   slices of bread and spread smoothly
   to sides. Put tops on. Wrap
   each sandwich in plastic and
                (cont'd)

Frozen Luncheon Sandwiches
(cont'd)

lay separately on cookie sheet.
Freeze. When frozen, you can
stack them.

The night before you want to serve the
sandwiches, crush the chips and set
aside. Beat milk and eggs together,
and put this in a flat-ish dish.
Dip frozen sandwiches (including
the edges) in this and then in chips.
Put on lightly greased cookie sheet.
Be sure to have plenty of chips on
top of each sandwich.

Keep in refrigerator on cookie sheet
    overnight to thaw.
When ready, bake at 300° for one hour.
Plop a sprig of fresh parsley on each
    top just before serving.

10 Sandwiches

Fish

You try this one – I'm scared to!

Wrap whole, cleaned fish securely
    in foil.
Put fish in your dishwasher - no
    soap, please!
Run dishwasher through its full
    cycle.
They say your fish will be
    perfectly cooked!

A good friend tells me this
    reminds her of the old one
    about cooking your pot
    roast tied to the manifold
    between SF and Tahoe!

24

Picnic Barbecue

When your relatives and all the children
  are coming, This is for you!

1 can corned beef, chopped
4 medium yellow onions, chopped
2 stalks celery, chopped
1 cup drained canned tomatoes
1 1/2 cups water
1 Tblsp. chili powder
1 Tblsp. vinegar
3 Tblsp Worcestershire sauce
1/4 cup chili sauce

Sauté onions and celery in a little oil
  until glossy.
Add all other ingredients and simmer
  very slowly, uncovered, 1 To 1 1/2
  hours. Add a little more water
  if it becomes too dry. Refrigerate.

Reheat and serve in warm hamburger
  buns.

Serves 6

25

Short Ribs

A much forgotten delicious dish!

4 TO 6 meaty short ribs
1 beef bouillon cube dissolved in
    ½ cup boiling water
1 can Tomato sauce (8 oz.)
½ cup red wine
2 Tablespoons vinegar
1 Tablespoon dried parsley flakes
1 Tablespoon wet mustard
1 Teaspoon horseradish (prepared Type)
1 large bay leaf, broken up
¼ cup chopped yellow onion
1 Teaspoon salt

Mix Together all ingredients except
    short ribs.
Put ribs in one layer in flat, oven-
    proof dish.
Pour on The marinade and let stand
    for several hours or all day.
    Turn ribs occasionally.
When ready, cover and place in 350°
    oven for 1 hour. Remove cover
    and Turn ribs. Bake uncovered
    ½ hour more.

Serves 4 —

26

Sausage and Veal

A family favorite!

½ lb. pork sausage
2 lbs. boneless veal cut in 2-inch cubes
1 cup all purpose flour
1 medium yellow onion, chopped
1 Teasp. paprika
½ Teasp. basil
¼ Teasp. Thyme
¾ cup dry white wine

Brown sausage lightly. Remove from
    pan.
Dredge veal with flour. Brown in
    sausage drippings. Pour off all
    excess grease.
Add sausage, onion, paprika, basil, and
    Thyme and place in 2-qt. casserole.
Pour wine over casserole, cover, and
    refrigerate.
When ready, bake, covered, at 350°
    for 1½ hours.

Serve over hot noodles using The
    delicious juice from casserole
    as gravy.
                    Serves 5

27

Teen Mix

A special favorite of Teenagers - who
consume this in quantity!

4 slices bacon
½ large yellow onion, chopped
1 lb. very lean ground beef
1 large can (1 lb., 12 oz.) baked beans, undrained
1 teasp. Worcestershire sauce
1 large can (1 lb., 12 oz.) solid pack tomatoes,
                                                undrained

⅛ teasp. garlic salt
1 heaping teasp. granulated sugar
   salt and pepper to taste

Cut bacon in strips and cook them with the
   onion in a large, heavy kettle like a Dutch
   oven. Do not brown bacon—it should be
   barely cooked.
Add ground beef and brown slightly. Drain off
   all excess grease.
Add remaining ingredients and stir gently.
Cover kettle and simmer 1¼ hours. Stir
   occasionally to prevent sticking.
This may be made ahead, refrigerated in a
   large bowl, and then reheated for
   4 to 6 hungry teenagers. Our adult
   children still love it!
Note: If you prefer it less juicy, do not
   use all the liquid with the tomatoes.

Deviled Crab

This one can be prepared a day ahead, too!

1/4 cube butter
1 large onion, minced
2 stalks celery, chopped fine
1 1/2 pounds crabmeat, shredded
2 or 3 slices bread, toasted and crumbled fine
1 Tblsp. Worcestershire sauce
  Dash cayenne
  Salt and pepper
1/2 Tsp. dry mustard
  mayonnaise

Fry onion and celery slowly in butter
  until glossy. Remove from flame.
Add crab
Mix together the Worcestershire, cayenne,
  salt, pepper, and mustard. Add to
  crab mixture.
Add enough mayonnaise to hold together.
Refrigerate in shells or small individual
  baking dishes.

When ready to bake, sprinkle with
  crumbs, dot with butter, and place
  in 400°-450° oven for 15 minutes.

Serves 6-8

Chicken Tamale

A real "company" dish!

3 Tamales cut into bite-size pieces
   (or use 2 jars)
1 cup canned Tomato pulp (drain solid
   pack Tomatoes well)
1 small can whole kernel corn
1 cup chopped or sliced olives (ripe)
½ cup chili sauce
1 Tblsp. olive or salad oil.
1 Tblsp. Worcestershire sauce
1 cup grated cheese
2 cups cooked chicken cut into
   good sized chunks (The equiva-
   lent of 1 large stew hen.)

Mix the above except cheese and
   store in casserole in refrigerator.

when ready to bake, cover with
   grated cheese and bake 1
   hour at 350°.

Serves 6 to 8

30

Quick Tamale

The family will love This

4 small cans chicken Tamale
2/3 can cream-style corn
1/2 can pitted olives, drained (ripe)
1/3 cup grated cheese

Combine Tamale, corn, and olives.
Sprinkle cheese on Top.
Refrigerate

When ready To bake, place in
      350° oven, uncovered, for
      40 minutes.

Serves 4

31

Covina Crab

A popular party dish!

5 pkgs. (6 oz. each) frozen crabmeat, Thawed
    Can use same amount canned or fresh.
12 hardboiled eggs, chopped
6 slices white bread
2 cups Half and Half
2 cups real mayonnaise
2 Teaspoons lemon juice
2 Tablespoons grated yellow onion
1 Tablespoon dried parsley flakes
1 can (4 oz.) pimientos, drained and chopped
1 can (8 oz.) mushrooms, drained
    salt and pepper To Taste
    Cornflakes, crushed

Trim crusts from bread and cube bread.
Combine all but Cornflakes and mix gently.
Place in large, greased casserole and
    refrigerate.
When ready, sprinkle Cornflakes all over
    The Top and bake for 1 hour at 300°,
    uncovered.

Serves 8 amply —

32

Top of the Stove Lamb Stew

A delicious winter meal!

1 clove garlic, minced
1/3 cup salad oil
1 1/3 lbs. lamb stew meat
   flour, salt, pepper
1 cup white wine
1/2 cup vermouth
1 cup water
4 carrots, peeled and cut in chunks
2 large Turnips (cut in half) or 4 small
      Turnips, peeled
2 yellow onions, peeled and halved
2 potatoes, peeled and cut in half
1 box (3½ oz.) fresh mushrooms, sliced

Lightly brown garlic in oil.
Shake lamb in bag containing flour, salt
      and pepper. Brown in the oil with
      garlic.
Cool (so it won't spatter) and add wines
      and water. Cover and simmer
      one hour, stirring occasionally.
Meanwhile prepare vegetables and put in
      plastic bag in refrigerator. Put
      potatoes in dish of cold water
      so they won't turn dark.

Cont'd.   33

Top of The Stove Lamb Stew (cont'd)

Refrigerate stew after simmering.

When ready, add vegetables (except
mushrooms) and simmer, covered,
for 40 minutes, adding mushrooms
The last 10 minutes.

If, at any Time you Think you need
more liquid, add wine.

Dinner for 4 —

34

Busy Day Dinner

When you have no time to prepare dinner
for the family, this is for you!

1 lb. very lean ground beef
1 pkg. stew vegetables (20 oz. found in
    section with frozen vegetables – in
    a cello sack)
1 can (10¾ oz.) Golden Mushroom soup –
    can use tomato or celery, etc., if you prefer.

Grease a 2-qt. casserole.

Break up half the meat and spread it
    in bottom of dish.

Scatter on half the vegetables.

Add half the soup (undiluted) and
    spread around.

Repeat all this.

Refrigerate, and when ready, place in
    325° oven, covered, for 2½ hours.
    Stir up gently half way through.
    If your dish does not have a top,
    use 2 layers of foil and tie with a
    string.

Simple! Serves 4 happy eaters or 3
    happy eaters with big appetites.

35

Chicken Bake

My husband chuckled at this because to him Half and Half is a brand of Tobacco.

1 good sized fryer, cut in pieces
2 eggs, beaten
About 2 cups of flour seasoned with salt and pepper
Margarine
1 cup Half and Half

Tip chicken pieces one by one in beaten eggs and then shake in paper bag containing the flour. Place in refrigerator covered with wax paper.

When ready to bake, lay side by side closely in baking dish or pan and dot with margarine. Add 2 slices of margarine to pan.

Place in 475° oven for 30 minutes. Tip the pan a time or two to spread the margarine on bottom of pan.

Pour Half and Half over chicken and bake one hour longer at 350°.

If chicken seems to be drying, you may add more Half and Half.

Be sure to let Half and Half reach room temperature, or it will crack a baking dish.

Serves 4

Dinner for One, please, James!

Put one fairly thick lamb chop (shoulder
   chop is fine) in small flat baking dish
   or small foil pie pan.
Spread chop with chutney.
Bake, uncovered, at 350° for about 40
   minutes.

And, a little fancier?

1 meaty chicken breast
   red wine (about 1/3 cup)
1/2 can (10 3/4-oz. can) cream of chicken soup
1 sandwich slice of Swiss cheese, cut in slivers
1/4 pkg. (3-oz. pkg.) smoked sliced beef, cut in
   slivers

In the morning (or night before) put
   chicken in baking dish as above,
   skin side down. Pour on wine and
   refrigerate.
When ready, turn chicken and spread
   undiluted soup over it.
Bake, uncovered, at 350° for one hour.
Spread beef over chicken and top with
   cheese. Spoon sauce over all well.
   Bake 15 minutes more.

37

Salmon Steaks

Fresh are best — if you can obtain them!

4 salmon steaks, 3/4" thick
1 lemon — for juice
1/2 teaspoon basil
  salt and pepper to taste
1/4 cup mayonnaise
3/4 cup commercial sour cream
4 green onions, chopped — including some
  of the green tops
1 lemon, sliced

Squeeze lemon juice generously on both
  sides of the steaks.
Sprinkle a little salt on bottom of a flat
  greased baking dish (helps prevent
  sticking) and lay steaks in dish.
  Refrigerate several hours.
Meanwhile combine basil, salt, pepper,
  mayonnaise and sour cream.
  Refrigerate this.
When ready, spread above mixture
  completely over steaks.
Scatter onions on top.
Bake, uncovered, at 350° for about 35
  minutes.
Serve with a thin slice of lemon on
  top of each steak.

Good with cucumbers on page 121.

A real treat for 4!

38

Spaghetti Sauce

Everyone has her favorite, and this is mine.
  Yes - I know you'll say I used everything
  but the kitchen sink!

2 lbs. lean ground beef
2 cloves garlic, minced
½ cup red wine
1 can mushrooms, undrained
1 pkg. dehydrated onion soup (1½ oz.)
2 teasp. crushed basil leaves
½ teasp. salt
¼ teasp. pepper
    large pinch cinnamon
    large pinch allspice
3 Tblsp. chopped fresh parsley
1 large can solid pack tomatoes, undrained
1 can tomato paste (6 oz. size)
1 cup water - more or less depending on
    the consistency you want.

Brown meat and garlic in large iron frying pan.
Add wine and simmer, stirring often, for 10
    minutes.
Add all remaining ingredients.
Cover pan almost completely (allowing space
    for steam to escape) and simmer 1 hour.
Toss with 12 oz. of steaming hot spaghetti
    and serve 8 hungry people.
This may be made ahead and refrigerated - or
    frozen - or just made when desired.

39

Crispy Chicken

Simple and Tasty for company or family.

1 chicken, cut in pieces
1/4 lb. butter, melted
1 pkg. Pepperidge Farm Stuffing
  (You really will need only 1/2 pkg. for
   1 chicken.)
Salt and pepper To Taste.

First roll out The stuffing with a
  rolling pin To make crumbs.

Then dip The chicken, piece by piece,
  in The butter and roll it untit
  covered in The stuffing crumbs.

Place in a shallow baking pan or on
  a cookie sheet and sprinkle with
  salt and pepper lightly. Refrigerate

When ready To bake, place in a 350°
  oven for 1 1/4 hours.

(For company use breasts, Thighs, and
  legs.)

Serves 4

Crab Supreme

Make it a day ahead!

8 slices bread
2 cups crabmeat
1 yellow onion, chopped
1/2 cup mayonnaise
1 cup celery, chopped
1/2 cup green pepper, chopped

4 eggs, beaten
3 cups milk
1 cup canned mushroom soup
grated cheese
paprika

Cook celery slowly 10 minutes in a little water. Drain.

Dice half of bread into baking dish.

Mix crab, onion, mayonnaise, pepper, and celery and spread over bread.

Dice other slices of bread and place over crab mixture.

Mix eggs and milk together and pour over dish.

Cover and place in refrigerator overnight.

Bake for 15 minutes at 325°. Then spoon soup over the top. Sprinkle top with cheese and paprika.

Bake one hour more or until golden brown.

Serves 8

Chinese Stroganoff

You make this yummy dish a day ahead!

1½ lbs. beef cut for stroganoff
⅛ cup salad oil
1 red Bermuda onion, chopped
½ cup green onions, sliced thin
1 can (8 oz.) bamboo shoots, drained
1 can (8½ oz.) water chestnuts, drained and sliced
4 oz. mushrooms, sliced
½ cup beef broth (make from cubes)
1 Tablespoon sugar
2 Tablespoons cornstarch
½ cup soy sauce
1 can (1 lb.) sliced freestone peaches un-drained

Brown meat in oil.
Add onions (both kinds), bamboo shoots, water chestnuts, mushrooms, broth and sugar. Cover and simmer 5 minutes.
Blend cornstarch with one Tablespoon water and the soy sauce. Add to mixture and simmer (stirring occasionally so it doesn't stick) until juice thickens.
Put in baking dish and refrigerate.
When ready to bake, pour peach juice over all, decorate with peaches, cover, and bake at 300° for 45 minutes or til hot through.

Serves 5

42

Egg-Asparagus-Mushroom Casserole

A wonderful Friday luncheon dish!

2 Tblsp. butter
3 Tblsp. flour
1/2 Teasp. prepared brown mustard
1 can mushroom soup.
1 large can green asparagus Tips
4 hardcooked eggs, sliced
1/2 cup rice-type cereal, crushed before
    measuring
1/4 cup grated American cheese

Melt butter, add flour, and blend well.
Combine mustard with soup and add To
    flour mixture. Cook slowly, stirring
    constantly, until Thick.
In a buttered casserole arrange a layer
    of half The drained asparagus, Then
    half The eggs and half The sauce.
    Repeat. Refrigerate - or set aside.
When ready, combine rice cereal and cheese
    and sprinkle over The Top.
Place in a 350° oven, uncovered, and bake
    until hot Through — about 35
    minutes.

Serves 4

Chicken Chili

A hot Tasty chicken dish!.

4 double chicken breasts, cooked in salted water

8-10 Tortillas (a Mexican food found in The refrigerator area of your market — or in a can)

2 cans mushroom soup, undiluted

1 can cream of chicken soup, undiluted

½ can beef broth, undiluted

1 yellow onion, chopped

1 can (about 7 oz.) green chile salsa (a sauce)

1 lb. Tillamook or cheddar cheese, grated salt and pepper To Taste

Remove chicken from bones in large bite-sized pieces.

Cut Tortillas in eighths.

Mix The 2 soups and broth and soak the Tortillas in This.

Put all in casserole in layers as listed above.

Refrigerate.

When ready To bake, place in 300° oven, uncovered, for 1 hour.

Stir up from bottom of casserole before serving.

(If you can't find green chili salsa, you may substitute red chile puree — both are Mexican foods.)

Serves 6 amply —

44

Meat Balls!

1½ lbs. ground round steak
1 pkg. dry onion soup mix
1 cup water
2 8-oz. cans tomato sauce
½ teasp. garlic salt
½ teasp. thyme
½ teasp. pepper
½ teasp. oregano
1 teasp. dehydrated parsley flakes

Set meat aside while you cook on top of
    the stove (for a very short time)
    the soup mix and water.
While this is simmering, open tomato
    sauce and pour about 2 Tblsp. of
    it into a cup. To this add the
    garlic salt, thyme, pepper, oregano,
    and parsley flakes. Stir it all
    well and then mix it thoroughly
    with the ground beef.
Add remaining tomato sauce to the
    simmering onion soup. Stir
    carefully.
Make beef mixture into meatballs the size
    of a small egg and place in a
    2-qt. casserole. Over this pour
    the sauce. Refrigerate, covered.
Bake at 350°, covered, for one hour.
Serve over spiced, or wild, or plain rice.
Makes about 20 meatballs.

45

Shrimp and Cheese Casserole

An all-Time favorite! Serve This at your next party, and you will agree.

6 slices white bread
1 pound prepared shrimp (ready To eat)
1/2 pound Old English cheese (usually comes sliced)
1/4 cup margarine or butter, melted
1/2 Teasp. dry mustard - salt To Taste
3 whole eggs, beaten
1 pint milk

Break bread in pieces about size of a quarter.
Break cheese into bite-size pieces.
Arrange shrimp, bread, and cheese in several layers in greased casserole.
Pour margarine or butter over This mixture.
Beat eggs. Add mustard and salt To eggs. Then add The milk. Mix Together and pour This over ingredients in casserole.
Let stand a minimum of 3 hours, preferably overnight in refrigerator, covered.

Bake one hour in 350° oven, covered.

Naturally if you slightly increase the amount of shrimp, you improve The dish - but it is fine "as is." When doubling The recipe, use 3 pounds of shrimp. Serves 4

46

Lamb Moussaka

An unusual Treat for 10!

3 lbs boneless lean lamb, cut for stew
1 cup flour
4 Tablespoons salad oil
1 medium yellow onion, chopped
2 cloves garlic, minced
1/2 cup red wine
1 can (16 oz.) whole Tomatoes, undrained
1 1/2 Teaspoons salt, 1 Teaspoon dried rose-
    mary, 2 Teaspoons dried parsley flakes
2 small eggplants, peeled and cut in 1 1/4" cubes
1/2 lb. fresh mushrooms, sliced

Shake lamb, a few pieces at a Time, in
    flour in paper bag.
Heat oil in large frying pan and brown
    meat well. Put meat in greased 5- or
    6-QT. casserole.
Slowly cook onions and garlic in pan
    drippings until glossy. Add a bit
    more oil if necessary. Stir To pick
    up all particles. Add To casserole.
Pour wine into pan and simmer a minute
    or so.
Add Tomatoes with juice (breaking up
    whole Tomatoes) and add seasonings.
    Cook, stirring often, for 5 minutes.
    Pour over lamb and refrigerate,
    covered.
                (cont'd)   47

Lamb Moussaka (cont'd)

Peel and cut eggplants and put
   in refrigerator in plastic bag.
Slice mushrooms and do likewise.

When ready to bake, add eggplants
   and mushrooms to casserole,
   Toss gently, and bake at
   350°, covered, for 1½ hours.
   Stir once half way through.

Captain's Casserole

A delicious double duty dish!

2 chicken fryers, cut in pieces
   a little flour, salt and pepper
1/2 lb. butter or margarine
1 large yellow onion thinly sliced
1 green pepper thinly sliced (remove membranes)
2 cans solid pack tomatoes (1 lb., 12 oz. each)
1/2 teasp. garlic powder
1 teasp. salt
1/2 teasp. pepper
1 tblsp. chopped parsley
1/2 teasp. thyme
1/2 teasp. oregano
1 heaping tblsp. curry powder

Sprinkle chicken with flour, salt, and
   pepper and fry quickly in butter until
   golden brown. Remove chicken.
Into the butter put onion and green pepper
   and fry slowly until glossy.
Mix remaining ingredients into undrained tomatoes,
   chopping tomatoes a bit. Add this to onions
   and peppers and simmer 5 minutes.
In a 3-qt. casserole arrange chicken, pour sauce
   over it and refrigerate until baking time.
Bake, covered, for 1 1/4 hours at 350°. Serve with
   white, wild, or brown rice to 8. Mustard
   pickle is a good accompaniment.
I freeze remaining sauce and use for soup base.

49

Pizza Pie

For the teenage cooks'.

1 lb. lean ground beef
1/2 tsp. salt
1/4 tsp. pepper
1 cup well drained canned tomatoes.
    Use a good brand which contains
    more tomatoes than juice.
1/2 cup freshly shredded sharp cheese
2 Tblsp. fine chopped onion
2 Tblsp. chopped parsley (cut with scissors)
1/4 teasp. dried basil
1/4 teasp. oregano

Mix beef with salt and pepper and
    pat out in a 9" pie plate.
Chop up tomatoes a bit and spread
    over meat. Sprinkle with re-
    maining ingredients.
Refrigerate.
When ready, bake in a 375° oven
    for 20-30 minutes.

Cut in wedges to serve 4 —

Stroganoff Bake

No last minute mixing in this Stroganoff.

6 slices bacon, cooked
2 pounds veal cut in large bite-size pieces
2 large yellow onions, chopped
½ pound fresh mushrooms
1 pint commercial sour cream
1 cup white cooking wine
1 cup raw white rice

Set cooked bacon aside and brown veal
   in bacon grease. Remove from pan.
Brown onions in pan.
Slice mushrooms.
Combine veal, onions, and mushrooms,
   and add the sour cream which you
   have mixed with wine.
Cover and cook slowly on top stove for
   2 hours. Stir occasionally.
Boil rice, drain, and combine with
   above mixture in layers. Refrigerate.
When ready to bake, crumble cooked
   bacon on top and bake, uncovered,
   at 300° for one hour or until
   piping hot.
Serves 6

Chicken, Coffee, Cheese!

What a combination, but just try it.

1 medium fryer, cut up — or 4 large half
    breasts
  salt, pepper, powdered ginger
  margarine
¼ cup Sauterne
1 can mushroom soup, undiluted
2 Tablespoons grated Parmesan-Romano cheese
1 Tablespoon instant coffee

Rub salt, pepper, and ginger into chicken.
Brown chicken in margarine.
Put chicken in one layer in flat baking dish.
Add wine, soup, cheese, and coffee to pan
    you browned chicken in, and stir well.
Pour sauce over chicken.
Refrigerate.
When ready, cover and bake at 325° for
    45 minutes. Baste and continue baking,
    covered, for 30 minutes more.

If you are having company, try this. Drain
    and wash in cold water 1 can deveined
    medium shrimp (4½ oz.) and heat in
    the sauce. Then serve the chicken
    and pour the sauce with shrimp
    over hot, fluffy white rice.

Serves 4

Rice and Deviled Eggs with Tuna

Deluxe and Inexpensive!

1/4 cup green pepper, chopped

1/4 cup minced onion

2 Tblsp. butter

1/2 cup milk

1 can mushroom soup

2 cups cooked rice

1 cup flaked tuna

3/4 cup grated cheddar cheese

1 cup bread crumbs, fried slowly in butter

6 deviled eggs

Cook green pepper and onions in butter until
    glossy.
Combine soup and milk.
To 3/4 of the soup mixture, add rice and tuna.
Place in casserole.
Top with deviled eggs and refrigerate.
When ready to bake, pour over remaining
    soup mixture and sprinkle with buttered
    crumbs and cheese.
Bake at 350° for 40 minutes.

Deviled Eggs

6 eggs, hardboiled

1/2 tsp. salt, 1/8 tsp. pepper, 1 tsp. wet mustard,
    1 tsp. horseradish

1 tsp. minced fresh parsley

1/4 cup mayonnaise

Cut eggs in half lengthwise. Mash yolk. Add
    other ingredients to yolks and mix well.
Fill egg whites.

Serves 6   53

Wild Rice Party Casserole

A special favorite!

2 cups boiling water
2/3 cup uncooked wild rice
1 can chicken rice soup
1 small can mushrooms, undrained
1/2 cup water
1 Teasp. salt
1 bay leaf
1/4 Teasp. each of celery salt, garlic salt,
   pepper, onion salt, and paprika.
3 Tblsp. chopped onion
3 Tblsp. salad oil
3/4 lb. lean ground beef

Pour boiling water over rice. Let stand,
   covered, 15 minutes. Drain.
Place rice in a 2-qt casserole.
Add soup, mushrooms with liquid, water,
   and seasonings. Mix gently and let
   stand a few minutes.
Sauté onions in oil until glossy. Remove
   and add to casserole.
Add meat to frying pan and fry, stirring
   gently until brown and crumbly.
Add to rice and refrigerate.
When ready, bake 2 hours at 325°, covered.
Serves 4

54

Sauce for Loaf on Preceding Page

Marvelous sweet-sour sauce!

This should be put together in order given.

1 Tablespoon flour
1/4 cup (2 oz.) butter or margarine
2 beef bouillon cubes — or 2 rounded
    teaspoons instant
1/2 cup boiling water
1/2 cup vinegar
8 Tablespoons wet mustard
1 1/2 cups sugar
2 egg yolks, well beaten

In the top of a double boiler, over gently
    boiling water, cream together the
    flour and butter. (A wire whisk makes
    all this easy.)
Dissolve beef bouillon in the boiling
    water and add, stirring, to the above.
Add the vinegar, mustard, and sugar, and
    lastly the eggs. (Add eggs very
    slowly, beating — so they don't cook!)
Continue cooking in double boiler, uncovered,
    about 20 minutes or until slightly
    thickened — stir occasionally.
This keeps well in refrigerator in covered jar.
Reheat, uncovered, in top of double boiler.

58

Chicken and Spaghetti

Takes 2 pages, but it's worth it!
And it can be frozen ⌣

8 chicken breasts
1/2 lb. spaghetti
3/4 lb. fresh mushrooms, washed, sliced, and
    sauteed in a little margarine
3 generous Tablespoons margarine
3 Tablespoons flour
1 1/2 cups stock — from cooking chicken
1/2 cup white wine
    salt to taste
1 cup heavy cream
1 lb. ham (the cooked slices) with skin
    and fat removed. Diced into about 1/4" cubes
2 pkgs. (2 1/2 oz. each) slivered almonds
3/4 cup grated Parmesan cheese
paprika

Simmer chicken in water until cooked thro'.
    Save water. Remove chicken from bones
    in large bite-sized pieces, discarding the
    skin. Cool stock and skim fat from top.
    Strain for later use. You can now re-
    frigerate all this overnight, pouring some
    of the stock on chicken to keep it tender.
The next day boil spaghetti about 8 minutes — in
    a large kettle. Drain into colander and
    run under cold water to prevent sticking.
    Cut a bit with a sharp knife for easier
    handling.

(cont'd) 55

Chicken and Spaghetti
cont'd

Sauté mushrooms in oleo and set aside.

Now make a sauce by melting the 3 tablespoons
of oleo and adding the flour. I use a wire
whip and add flour slowly, stirring to keep
as smooth as possible. Then add the 1½
cups stock, using the same method. Cook
very slowly until it thickens, stirring
often.

Remove from heat and add wine, salt, and cream.
Mix gently.

Put spaghetti into your large kettle, add
cream sauce, chicken (minus stock if
it was in it in the refrigerator), ham,
mushrooms and nuts. Mix all well and
put in a large, greased casserole.

Cover with cheese and sprinkle with paprika.
This now can be frozen, covered tightly.
Thaw before baking by moving to refrigerator
the night before.
Or put in refrigerator until ready to bake that
evening at 350°, uncovered, for 45 minutes.
Use remaining stock in soup — or freeze in
ice cube trays and put in plastic bag
in freezer.

Serves 10-12

56

Adella Loaf
A perfect party dish!

1 lb. pre-cooked ham, ground (cut
    fat first)
1 lb. very lean ground pork sausage
1 lb. very lean ground round
1 ½ cups milk
2 eggs, slightly beaten
1 cup (generous) dry seasoned stuffing
    mix — roll fine with a rolling
    before measuring
pepper to taste
1 can (10¾ oz.) condensed tomato
    soup, undiluted

Mix all together and put in greased
    loaf pans or 3-qt. baking dish
    (deep, not flat) and refrigerate.
When ready, bake at 350°, uncovered,
    for 2 hours.
Serve with sauce on following page.

(The friend who gave me this recipe — and
who is a super cook — surrounds her
loaf, when serving, with warm fruit.
Delicious — and attractive looking!.)

Serves 10 —

57

Family Dinner for Four

Meat, potatoes, and vegetables, all in one!

1 lb. lean ground chuck
   salt and pepper to taste
4 medium sized potatoes
   sliced onions, according to your taste
1/2 Teasp. Worcestershire Sauce
1 large can solid pack Tomatoes

Brown the meat with the onions and add
   salt and pepper.
Peel potatoes and slice them into a 2-qt.
   casserole.
Place meat and onions on top of potatoes.
Add Worcestershire to the Tomatoes -
   do not drain them - and pour
   This over all.
Refrigerate.

When ready to bake, place in 350° oven
   covered, for 1 1/2 hours or until potatoes
   are done.
Note: If you want to be fancier, you
   may add 2 cups diced celery and
   1/2 cup diced green pepper. Arrange
   in layers with the potatoes.

Serves 4

59

Chicken
And it's Tasty!

1/3 cup flour
   salt and pepper
4 chicken breasts
1/2 cup salad oil
1 yellow onion, chopped
1 clove garlic, minced
1 can (6 oz.) tomato paste
3/4 cup white wine
1 can (4 oz.) mushrooms and juice
1 Tablespoon chopped parsley

Put flour, salt and pepper in paper bag
   and shake chicken in this, one
   piece at a time.
Heat salad oil and brown chicken.
   Remove chicken and put in one
   layer in baking dish. (I use 8" x 8")
Simmer garlic and onion in oil until
   onion is glossy.
Add tomato paste, wine, and mushrooms.
   Stir all and bring to a boil. Pour
   over chicken and refrigerate.
When ready, sprinkle with parsley and
   bake, covered (can use foil) for
   1 1/4 hours at 350°.

Serves 4

60

Beans!

There are loads of recipes for beans,
  but this one is "extra special!"

2 cloves garlic, minced
3 medium yellow onions, thinly sliced
4 Tablespoons salad oil or bacon grease
1 No. 2½ can pork and beans (about 1 lb., 14 oz.)
1 No. 2 can red kidney beans (about 1 lb., 4 oz.)
1 No. 2 can small green lima beans
½ cup brown sugar
¼ cup vinegar
½ cup ketchup
1 Teaspoon mustard (wet or dry)
1 Teaspoon salt

Fry garlic and onions in oil until glossy.
Drain kidney and lima beans
Mix all ingredients well and pour into
  2-qt. baking dish or bean pot.
Refrigerate.
When ready to bake, place in 350°
  oven for 1 – 1¼ hours.
Cover if you want lots of juice, other-
  wise bake uncovered.
Stir well just before baking.

Serves 8

Curried Shrimp
Quick and Tasty!

1 can Cream of Mushroom soup
1 4-oz. can mushrooms, undrained
1/2 Tsp. Worcestershire
1/4 Tsp. dry mustard
1/2 Tsp. curry powder
1/8 Tsp. pepper
3/4 lb. fresh cooked shrimp - or 2 or 3
    cans, drained and washed.
1/2 cup slivered almonds, Toasted lightly
    in a little butter

Mix soup, undrained mushrooms, and
    seasonings.
Add shrimp. Refrigerate.
(You can use leftover lamb or poultry.)

To serve, heat in Top of double boiler
    until piping hot. Add nuts.

Serve over hot fluffy white rice - with
    a fruit salad.

Have plenty of chutney on hand when
    serving curry!

Serves 4 —

62

Cambridge Chicken with Ham

Another "day ahead" one!

1 large fryer, cut in pieces
   flour, mixed with a little salt and pepper
¼ lb. butter or margarine
¼ cup chopped green onions
1 4-oz. can mushrooms, drained
1 slice ham, diced
1 clove garlic, minced
   pinch of thyme
   salt and pepper to taste
1 cup red wine

Shake chicken piece by piece in a paper bag containing the flour.

Brown chicken in butter and place in casserole.

Mix together all the remaining ingredients and pour over chicken. Spoon the juice over the chicken so it is well saturated.

Bake, covered, in a 350° oven for 1 hour.

Remove and cool for a short time before placing in the refrigerator overnight.

The next day, when ready to bake, again spoon the liquid over the chicken and place, covered, in a 300° oven for 1 hour.

Serves 4

63

Friday Favorite

Quick, easy, and delicious!

2 lbs. skinned Haddock fillets
Dijon mustard
salt and pepper to taste
½ cup cracker crumbs (the square
    small white type) seasoned
    with ¼ teasp. salt, ¼ teasp.
    pepper, ⅛ teasp. oregano or
    thyme.
Parsley
Lemon

Spread fillets lightly with mustard
    on both sides.
Sprinkle with salt and pepper.
Roll in cracker crumbs.
Refrigerate.

Heat oven to 500°.
Grease flat baking dish and heat thoroughly.
Lay fish in dish and bake at 500° for 10
    minutes.
Decorate with sprigs of parsley and serve
    with lemon wedges.

Serves 4 or 5. 64

Quiche

Served often by a NYC bachelor who
is a great cook!

1 pie shell (9") uncooked
1/2 lb. Swiss cheese, finely diced
1/2 lb. ham, finely cubed
5 whole eggs
1 cup Half and Half
1/4 Teaspoon salt
    several dashes nutmeg

Fill shell a little more than half full
    with alternating layers of cheese
    and ham. Refrigerate.
Beat together the eggs, cream, and salt.
    Refrigerate separately.
When ready, stir egg mixture with a
    fork and pour over pie. Sprinkle
    with nutmeg.
Bake at 400° for 15 minutes. Turn oven
    to 325° for 30 minutes. Cool 10
    minutes and serve promptly.
    Follow recipe exactly — or it may
    get soggy if it stands too long
    out of the oven.
This is really delicious, and actually
    it makes more than enough for
    9" pie shell.

Serves 4 ——

65

Biscuit Pie

Perfect for the family on a cold winter night!

3 Tablespoons margarine
4 Tablespoons salad oil
2 lbs. round steak, cut in pieces
   salt, pepper, and flour
2 cans (8 oz. each) mushrooms, drained
1/2 Teaspoon dried rosemary
1 Teaspoon dried parsley
1/2 Teaspoon dried thyme
1 bay leaf, broken up
1 1/2 cups Rosé wine
1 Tablespoon red wine vinegar
1 beef bouillon cube dissolved in 1/2 cup boiling water
1 can (14 oz.) artichoke hearts, drained
1 pkg. refrigerated biscuits
   melted butter
   grated Parmesan cheese
   paprika

Melt margarine in heavy frying pan.
Add salad oil.
Shake meat in a paper bag with salt, pepper, and
   flour — a few pieces at a time.
Brown meat in margarine and oil.
Add mushrooms, seasonings, 1 cup of the wine, vinegar
   and bouillon.
Simmer over very low heat for 1 1/2 hours, covered.
Add artichokes and put in casserole.
Refrigerate.
When ready to bake, add remaining wine, stir
   all gently and reheat, covered, for 30 minutes
   at 350°.
Turn oven to 400°. Dip biscuits, one by one, in melted
   butter — then in cheese — and put on top. Sprinkle
   them with paprika, and bake, uncovered, for
   8-10 minutes or until biscuits are done.

Serves 6

66

Easy Chicken in Wine

You don't even brown the chicken!

3 or 4 whole chicken breasts, cut in halves
1 cup Burgundy wine
1/4 cup soy sauce
1/4 cup salad oil
2 Tablespoons water
1 garlic clove, minced or mashed
1 Teaspoon powdered ginger
1/4 Teaspoon oregano leaves (crush be-
    tween your hands)
1 Tablespoon brown sugar

Place chicken breasts in one layer
    in shallow baking pan.
Mix together all other ingredients.
Pour sauce over chicken.
Cover with foil.
Refrigerate. (If you leave it all day,
    it helps to spoon sauce over it
    a couple of times.)
When ready to bake, again spoon
    sauce over chicken, and bake
    at 350° for 1 hour, covered.
    Remove foil, baste, and con-
    tinue baking 15 minutes more,
    uncovered.
Serves 6

67

Rice and Shrimp Casserole

An entirely differently flavored shrimp dish, and so good!

2 pounds shrimp - or 1 pound already cooked and prepared
1/3 cup onion, chopped and browned in
2 Tblsp. margarine
1 or 2 cloves minced garlic
1 cup raw white rice
1 large can Tomatoes, not drained
2 cups chicken bouillon
1 bay leaf broken in pieces
3 Tblsp. chopped parsley
1/2 Tsp. ground cloves
1/2 Tsp. Marjoram
1 Tsp. chili powder
dash cayenne
1 Tsp. salt
1/8 Tsp. pepper

Combine onion, garlic, rice, bay leaf, parsley, cloves, marjoram, chili powder, cayenne, salt, and pepper in casserole. Mix gently.
Combine Tomatoes and bouillon.

Just before baking, add wet ingredients to dry, add shrimp, and mix.
Bake 1 1/2 hours at 350°, covered.

Serves 6

Greco

Inexpensive and different!

1 yellow onion, chopped
1 green pepper, chopped
1 or 2 small cans mushrooms, drained
2 cups shell macaroni
3 cans tomato sauce
1 can cream style corn
   sharp cheese
1 pound ground round or chuck

Fry onion and green pepper in
   small amount of oil until glossy.
Brown ground meat in above. Keep
   moving to prevent burning.
Add mushrooms and remove from heat.
Boil macaroni until tender. Drain
   and add to above.
Add tomato sauce and corn and
   mix all well.
Place in greased casserole and
   refrigerate.

When ready to bake, grate lots of
   sharp cheese on top and place
   in 300° oven for 1 hour.

Serves 6

69

Easy Chicken with Onions

A delectable dish given to me by another
Navy wife. You will use it happily often.

6 "meaty" chicken breasts
12 to 16 tiny whole white onions, peeled.
    If you are really in a rush, buy a
    buffet can of onions. It is an 8'12-oz.
    can and contains 10 to 12 onions.
1 can Cream of Mushroom soup.
1/8 cup sherry - or more
1/4 lb. cheddar cheese - freshly grated

Place chicken in baking dish.
Add onions.
Mix soup and sherry. Pour over chicken.
Grate cheese over top. Refrigerate.

When ready, place in 350° oven, covered,
    for 45 minutes. Uncover and continue
    baking for a good 30-45 minutes
    more.

(Somewhere along the line I usually
    add some salt and pepper.)

Serves 6

70

Crab and Spinach Casserole

Just right for luncheon or buffet supper.

2 pkgs. frozen chopped spinach
1 pound crabmeat
1 1/2 cups grated sharp cheese
1 cup finely chopped onions
1 can tomato paste
1 cup commercial sour cream
   dash nutmeg
   salt and pepper

Thaw spinach.
Grate cheese.
Start with layer of spinach, then
   onions, then crab, then cheese.
   Add nutmeg, salt, and pepper.
   Repeat once again. Refrigerate.
When ready to bake, put mixture
   of sour cream and tomato paste
   on top.
Bake 45 minutes in 325° oven.

Serves 4.

71

Beef Brisket
Best done a day ahead!

4 cans (8 oz. each) Tomato sauce
1/4 cup chopped yellow onion
1 can (4 oz.) mushrooms with liquid.
3 to 4 lbs. beef brisket
1 pkg. dehydrated onion soup

Mix Tomato sauce with onions. Pour
   half of this into bottom of roasting
   pan.
Add mushrooms and liquid.
Place meat on top of all.
Sprinkle onion soup on top of meat.
Cover with remaining sauce.

Bake, covered, at 325° for 3 hours.
   Baste occasionally to keep top
   from drying out.
Refrigerate, covered, overnight. This
   thickens the sauce.

This is fine, sliced, on a hot summer
   night. But if you prefer it
   warm, reheat in very slow oven
   Serve sauce over rice.

Serves 8 or more —   72

Luncheon Dish
for the ladies!

2 cups diced cooked chicken or turkey
2 cans (4½ oz. each) chopped ripe olives
1 can (8 oz.) mushrooms, drained
¼ cup chopped onion
½ cup real mayonnaise
1 can (10¾ oz.) cream of chicken soup,
                      undiluted
1 cup commercial sour cream
6 slices white bread (regular, not thin sliced)

Trim crusts from bread and cut into
    ½" cubes.
Mix all and put in shallow greased
    baking dish. (I use 7½" x 12")
    Refrigerate.
When ready, cover with foil and
    bake at 300° for one hour.

Serves 8

73

Lobster Newburg

You can keep the makings for this
on your pantry shelf! Serves 6.

1 can lobster
1 can crabmeat
1 can shrimp
4 Tblsp. butter
1/2 Teasp. paprika
1/4 Teasp. nutmeg
2 cans Cream of Mushroom soup
1 can (3 oz.) sliced mushrooms - save juice
1 can evaporated milk - regular size
1/4 Teasp. salt
1/4 cup sherry

Melt butter in large skillet.
Wash seafood and sauté it in the
    butter for about 5 minutes.
Sprinkle on the paprika and nutmeg
    and stir a bit.
Mix together the soup, mushrooms (in-
    cluding liquid from can) and milk.
    Pour this over seafood.
Add salt and mix all gently. Simmer
    for 10 minutes. Stir occasionally to
    prevent sticking.
Refrigerate in large bowl.
Reheat in top of double boiler, uncovered.
When piping hot, add sherry and serve
    over rice, in patty shells, or on toast.

74

Cheesy Spinach Main Dish

with no noodles, no rice, no potatoes!

1 lb. very lean ground beef
1 Tablespoon salad oil
1 Teaspoon each salt, pepper, garlic powder
1 yellow onion, finely chopped
1/2 lb. fresh mushrooms, sliced
1 can (8 oz.) Tomato sauce
1 carton (8 oz.) commercial sour cream
1 Teaspoon each basil and oregano, crushed
8 oz. cottage cheese
2 pkgs. (10 oz. each) frozen chopped spinach, thawed
1/2 cup grated Parmesan cheese
1/2 cup grated Longhorn cheese
1/3 cup grated Parmesan cheese
1/2 cup grated Longhorn cheese

Brown meat in oil, stirring to prevent burning. Sprinkle on salt, pepper, and garlic powder.
Add onions and mushrooms and cook over low heat about 5 minutes, stirring occasionally. Drain off any excess liquid.
In a large bowl combine the tomato sauce, sour cream, basil, and oregano. Stir in the cottage cheese. Add all this to meat mixture.
Put thawed spinach in colander and press out all the liquid. Add spinach to above.
Add 1/2 cup Parmesan and 1/2 cup Longhorn. Mix in.
Put all in greased 9" x 13" flat baking dish and cover top with remaining cheeses. Refrigerate.
When ready, bake uncovered, at 350° for 30 minutes or 'til hot through.

Serves 5 to 6 —

Summer Main Dish Party Salad

A delicious salad made a day ahead!

2 cups real mayonnaise
2 Tablespoons lemon juice
2½ Tablespoons Chinese Type soy sauce
1 heaping Tablespoon curry powder
1 Tablespoon onion juice (or finely grated)
1 Tablespoon chutney
3 cups chicken or Turkey, cooked and cut
    in chunks (or 1½ cups crabmeat and
    1½ cups shrimp)
1½ cups chopped celery
1 can (6 oz.) water chestnuts, drained and
    sliced
2 cups seedless grapes
1 can (15¾ oz.) pineapple chunks, drained
1 pkg. (5½ oz.) slivered almonds, toasted in
    butter or margarine, and salted

Mix Together the mayonnaise, lemon
    juice, soy sauce, curry powder,
    onion juice and chutney.
Assemble all other ingredients except
    the nuts. Toss all This well in
    The mayonnaise mixture.
Place in refrigerator overnight so flavors
    will blend.
Just before serving, add nuts and toss again.
(Great on a heart of artichoke or avocado half!)

Best for a luncheon — Serves 8

76

Surprising Pork Chops

Hard To guess The ingredients!

Pork chops — ½" Thick
Equal amounts of Tomato ketchup and
     Coke (or Pepsi or Tab)

Trim excess fat from chops and brown
     on both sides. Put in one layer
     in baking dish
Mix sauce and pour over chops.
Bake, covered, at 350° for 40 minutes
     or more — 'Til chops are done.
     Peek occasionally and add more
     sauce if it is becoming dry.
     (Bake a bit longer if you do This.)

For 2 large chops (1½" Thick) I use
     ½ cup ketchup and ½ cup Coke,
     Pepsi, or Tab — in an 8" x 8" flat
     baking dish. Double sauce for
     4 chops.

Not really a "Make-ahead", but it's so
     simple To do!

Crab in Cups

Make a day ahead!

4 Tblsp. butter, melted
4 Tblsp. flour
1 Tsp. wet mustard
1 Tsp. salt
1 Tsp. Worcestershire
Dash cayenne

1 cup canned tomatoes, drained
1 cup mellow grated cheese
2 eggs, slightly beaten
1 1/2 cups milk
2 cups crabmeat in chunks

Blend flour into melted butter. Add next seven
ingredients. Cook slowly, stirring often,
about 5 minutes or until cheese melts.

Heat milk
Add seasoned ingredients to milk.
Add crab.
Let thicken in top of double boiler. Stir
occasionally. Refrigerate.

Reheat, uncovered, and serve in toast cups -
with a little parsley and paprika on top.

Toast Cups

Rub muffin tins with margarine.
Decrust sliced bread. Push into cups.
Bake at 275° until golden brown.
Reheat on cookie sheet.

Serves 6

78

Filet Steaks

This Time They're baked!

Steaks — Filet Mignon — one inch Thick
Butter or margarine

Brown filets quickly on both sides — in
hot skillet. Remove immediately
To a flat baking pan and set aside
away from The stove. Steaks should
not be touching.

Top each steak with a pat of butter or
margarine.

when ready, place in 325° oven for
15 minutes. Serve right away.
(If your steaks are 1½" Thick,
bake for 18 minutes.) Thickness
is important. I measure
with a ruler.

These are medium rare.

The onions at The bottom of p. 121
are good with These.

Sausages and Apples

Even your children will love this!

2 large or 3 small very tart apples
   brown sugar
1 cup long grain raw white rice
1 pkg. best quality link sausages
    (not the precooked ones)
1/4 cup ketchup

Core and slice apples but do not peel.
Cover bottom of 2-qt. casserole with apples.
Cover apples with brown sugar.
Boil rice according to pkg. directions.
Cover apples and sugar with rice.
Pour some boiling water over sausages
    and let stand 3 minutes. Drain.
    (This absorbs grease.)
Arrange sausages close together on rice.
Frost with ketchup and refrigerate.
When ready, bake at 350°, covered, for
    45 minutes to one hour. Uncover
    last 15 minutes.

Serves 4 —

Southern Chicken

Here we mean "South of the border!"

8 chicken breasts
4 cups cooked white rice
1 pint sour cream
1/2 cup mayonnaise
1 can (6 oz.) chopped green chiles, drained
1 lb. Monterey Jack cheese, shredded – or
    cut in tiny pieces.
1/4 teasp. garlic salt
2 pkgs. (4 oz. each) shredded cheddar cheese

Pull off skin and simmer chicken until
    cooked through. (Takes longer than
    you think.) Remove meat from
    bones in bite-size pieces.

Carefully mix all else together thorough-
    ly – except cheddar – adding chicken

Put in greased baking dish and cover
    Top with cheddar.

Refrigerate.

When ready, bake at 350°, covered, for
    30 minutes. Uncover and bake 30
    more minutes. Should be bubbly
    hot.

Serves 8 amply –

Clams in Shells

Make the night before and store in refrigerator. Makes 5 shells.

5 Tblsp. flour
4 Tblsp. butter
2 cans minced clams, drained — save juice
4 egg yolks beaten until light
2 Tblsp. chopped fresh parsley
2 Teasp. chopped onion
    salt and cayenne
    buttered crumbs

Make thick white sauce with flour, butter, and juice of clams.

When thoroughly blended (use wire whip) add egg yolks slowly, by teaspoon at first, so they won't string.

Add parsley, onion, pinch of salt and cayenne.

Mix in drained clams.

Place in shells and sprinkle with crumbs which you have toasted in a little butter. Refrigerate.

Put shells in pan with warm water to cover bottom of shells and brown in 375° oven 20-25 minutes.

Cays Firehouse Special

The men at the firehouse have great
fun cooking — and they like it hot!

1½ lbs. lean ground beef
1½ yellow onions, chopped
1 Tablespoon salad oil — or more
1 can (15 oz.) kidney beans, undrained
1 can (1 lb.) solid pack tomatoes, well drained
3 oz. bottled taco sauce
3 Tablespoons chili powder
1 can (4½ oz.) sliced olives, drained
1 pkg. (4 oz.) shredded cheddar cheese
1 medium pkg. corn chips
shredded lettuce
2 cups commercial sour cream

In large frying pan brown beef and onions in
   oil. Drain well.
Add beans, tomatoes, taco sauce, chili powder
   and olives. Stir gently and simmer
   for about 15 minutes, uncovered.
In the bottom of a 3-qt. baking dish, put
   half the meat mixture. Sprinkle with
   half the cheese. Cover with corn chips.
   Repeat — however, if baking later, omit
   top layer of chips when refrigerating.
When ready to bake, place in 350° oven,
   covered, for 45 minutes. (Remember
   your top layer of chips if necessary.)
Let stand 5 minutes out of oven, top with
   layer of lettuce and lastly a layer
   of sour cream — serve!

Serves 6 —

83

Not Navy Beans

The best you ever ate!

1 pkg. dry red kidney beans - 1 lb. size
1 clove garlic, minced
1 ham end with plenty of meat on the
   bone - at least 3 lbs.
1 bottle chili sauce
½ bottle ketchup

Soak the beans overnight.
The next morning drain the beans, place
   them in a kettle, and cover them with
   water.
Add the garlic.
Add ham end, skin and all.
Simmer beans until they begin to soften -
   about 3 hours. Add water if necessary
   during cooking to keep beans covered. Don't
   worry if beans burst!
Remove ham end. Take off the skin. Remove
   meat from bone and cut in large bite-size
   chunks. Return chunks to the beans.
   Simmer one hour more.
Drain beans except for about 1 cup bean liquor.
Add chili and ketchup to beans and mix gently.
Reheat slowly about 20 minutes until piping hot.
May be refrigerated and reheated - but keep it
   moist by adding more ketchup. Heat slowly!
Serves 6 to 8

84

Lobster Sturdevant

Serve this on a hot, sultry night in shells or ramekins with a green salad and corn pudding. It is just right!

Cheese glass (5 oz.) of real mayonnaise
A little less than a cheese glass of ketchup
½ jigger of chives (cut fine with scissors)
½ cup lemon juice
Lots of paprika (about 1 tsp.)
1 jigger brandy
1 lb. prepared lobster or crabmeat

Mix and store in refrigerator.
Serve cold.

These are certainly unusual directions, but this is the way it was told to me!

Serves 4 ~

85

Baked Salad

Make it, bake it, and serve it hot for
buffet supper- or make it, don't bake
it and serve it on lettuce for luncheon-
or make it, bake it, serve it, and place
remainder in refrigerator for a delectable
leftover. No matter what, it's extra-special!

1 cup chopped green pepper
½ cup chopped yellow onion
2 cups chopped celery
2 cups real mayonnaise
2 cans crabmeat (approximately 2 cups)
2 cans shrimp, drained   "   "   "
1 can lobster
1 can chunk or solid pack Tuna
1 Tsp. Worcestershire
1 Tsp. salt
   pepper to taste
   dash of Tabasco
   potato chips for topping

Mix all gently except chips. Refrigerate.
Crush chips and put on top.
Bake at 350° for ½ hour or until
   hot through.

Can be made a day ahead as marinating
   improves flavor!
Serves 6. Double for a luncheon for
   12 or dinner for 10.

86

Lamb Chops

Expensive, but delicious!

2 double thick small loin lamb chops per
    person
    slice of yellow onion for each chop
    slice of lemon for each chop
    chili sauce

Place chops in flat, greased baking dish in
    one layer.

Peel onion.

Do not slice onion or lemon too thick.

Put slice of onion on each chop — then
    lemon on top of onion — then a
    generous teaspoon of chili sauce
    on top of lemon.

Refrigerate.

When ready to bake, place in 340°
    oven, uncovered, for 1 hour.

Chinese Casserole

The unusual flavor and crunchiness of This dish give it a personality all its own.

2 cans solid pack Tuna
1 can mushroom soup
1/4 cup water
1 Tblsp. soy sauce
1 cup whole cashew nuts
1 4-oz. can button mushrooms, drained
2 cups canned Chinese Chow Mein noodles
1/4 cup minced onion or chopped green onion Tops
1 cup chopped celery

Drain Tuna and break it into bite size chunks.
Mix Together The mushroom soup, water, and soy sauce.
Combine Tuna, mushroom soup mixture, and all remaining ingredients except 1 cup of The noodles.
Mix gently and place in casserole.
Refrigerate.

When ready To bake, sprinkle remaining cup of noodles on Top and bake at 375°, uncovered, for 40 minutes.

Serves 6

88

Chinese Veal Casserole for Ten

Flavorful and different!

1 cup chopped yellow onions
3 lbs. boneless veal steak (or shoulder) cut
    in 1 inch cubes
2 Tablespoons salad oil
2 cups sliced celery
1 cup uncooked white rice
1 can (8 oz.) mushrooms, drained
1 can mushroom soup, undiluted
1 can cream of chicken soup, undiluted
4 cups water
1/2 cup soy sauce
1 Teaspoon salt
1 1/2 Teaspoons pepper
1 package (10 oz.) frozen peas, thawed
1 cup slivered almonds

Sauté onions and meat in oil until brown.
    Put in large casserole.
Mix in celery, rice, mushrooms, both
    soups, water, soy, salt and pepper.
Cover and bake at 350° for 45 minutes.

Refrigerate.

When ready to bake, stir in peas. Now
    bake, covered, at 350° for 30 minutes.
Uncover, sprinkle almonds on top and
    continue baking 15 minutes more
    or until hot through.

Chicken and Bean Sprouts

How's this for an unusual combination?

4 chicken breasts, skinned
1 can (8½ oz.) quartered artichoke hearts
    salt to taste
1 can (16 oz.) bean sprouts — less ⅓ cup
1 can (10½ oz.) cream of chicken soup, un-
    diluted
¼ cup dry vermouth
1 pkg. (4 oz.) shredded cheddar cheese
½ teasp. paprika

Simmer breasts until cooked through.
    Remove meat from bones.
Drain artichoke hearts and put in bottom
    of 1½ quart greased casserole.
Then the chicken — and salt to taste.
Drain bean sprouts and rinse them in a
    large strainer under cold water.
    (Remember to remove ⅓ cup) Add to dish.
Mix soup and vermouth and spread over all.
Top with cheese mixed with paprika.
Refrigerate.
When ready, bake at 350° for 40 minutes.
When serving, be sure to dig to the bottom
    to get all the goodies!

Serves 4 —   89

Pork Chops and Rice
So good!

4 center cut pork chops, 3/4" thick
   salt and pepper to taste
5 chicken bouillon cubes - or 5 teaspoons of
   powdered instant chicken bouillon
3 cups boiling water
1 can (10½ oz.) tomato puree
5 green onions, minced
1 can (4 oz.) mushrooms, drained
2 teaspoons liquid smoke flavoring
1 cup regular rice

Cut excess fat from chops. Place in
   8" x 12" flat baking dish.
Add salt and pepper and refrigerate if
   baking later.
When ready, dissolve bouillon cubes in water.
In a large bowl mix bouillon, tomato puree,
   onions, mushrooms and liquid smoke.
   Pour over chops.
Sprinkle rice over all, being sure it is
   all in contact with liquid mixture.
Bake at 350°, uncovered, for 1½ hours.

Good with pears on page 122.

for 4

93

Sophisticated Stew

A real "company" dish!

3 lbs. lean round or chuck cut into large
    bite size pieces
  paper bag of flour seasoned with salt
    and pepper
6 strips of bacon
2 cloves of garlic, finely minced
1 oz. brandy, warmed
12 small whole fresh mushrooms
1 cup condensed beef bouillon
1½ cups dry red wine
12 small peeled white onions
12 small carrots, sliced
6 slightly bruised peppercorns
4 whole cloves
1 bay leaf, crumbled
2 Tblsp. chopped fresh parsley
¼ Teasp. dried marjoram
¼ Teasp. Thyme

Shake beef cubes in the flour, a few at
  a time until they are well covered.
In a large iron skillet fry the bacon
  until it begins to brown but is not crisp.
  Cut bacon into one inch pieces after
  cooking. Place in earthenware or heavy
  glass baking dish.
Cont'd

Sophisticated Stew (Cont'd)

Cook the garlic a little in the bacon fat.

Then add the floured beef cubes and brown quickly on all sides, turning often.

Pour the brandy into the skillet, light it, and when flame dies out, remove the meat and garlic and put them in the casserole. (Garlic has probably disappeared by now.)

Put the mushrooms in skillet and brown lightly. Add them to casserole.

Put the bouillon and one cup of the red wine into skillet - bring to a boil and stir from the bottom to loosen the particles, using a wire whip. Pour the liquid into the casserole.

Add to the casserole the onions, carrots, peppercorns, cloves, bay leaf, parsley, marjoram, and thyme.

Now pour over the casserole your remaining ½ cup of red wine.

Cover the casserole tightly and bake at 300° for 2 hours. Cool, and place in refrigerator, covered.

When ready the next day, spoon some of the liquid up from the bottom over the meat and again place the casserole in a 300° oven, covered, and bake for 1 hour or until piping hot.

Serves 6

Veal Vermouth

Somewhat like a Veal Stew - very tasty!

2 lbs. veal cutlets, cut into serving size
        pieces - or a little smaller
    salt and pepper to taste
    Parmesan cheese (finely grated)
    Butter or margarine
2 large onions, chopped
4 or 5 carrots, sliced - not too thin
1 cup mushrooms, sliced (about ½ lb.)
3 chicken bouillon cubes
1½ cup boiling water
½ cup Vermouth or any white wine

Sprinkle cutlets with salt, pepper, and
        cheese.
Brown them in butter in a heavy skillet.
Place them in a 3-qt. casserole.
Now sauté the onions, carrots, and
        mushrooms in the skillet. Add more
        butter if necessary.
Meanwhile dissolve bouillon cubes in water
        and add wine. Pour over the semi-
        cooked vegetables. Then pour all over
        veal. Refrigerate casserole.
Bake, covered, at 325° for one hour.
Serves 5.
Juice is excellent over noodles, rice, or
        mashed potatoes.   22

                                            96

Clam and Corn Soufflé

A real Taste Teaser. No one will guess
what is in it!

1 1/4 cup crumbled soda crackers
1 cup milk
2 eggs, beaten
1 can minced clams, undrained
1 cup frozen corn, thawed but not cooked
3 Tblsp. melted butter
2 Tblsp. minced onion
1/4 Teasp. salt
1/2 Teasp. Worcestershire
1/2 cup shredded sharp cheese

Soak crackers until soggy in milk
    and beaten eggs (about 1/2 hour?)
Then add all but cheese.
Mix gently and refrigerate in a 1 1/2-qt.
    casserole.
When ready to bake, place casserole,
    uncovered, in 300° oven for
    50 minutes.
Sprinkle cheese on top and allow it to
    bake just long enough to melt
    cheese — about 10 minutes.

Good with Molded Salad on p. 123
                    Serves 4   97

Sausage Casserole for Six

Your family will love this, and for company
  serve it with dry red wine, green salad,
  and French bread.

1 pound pork sausage (not highly seasoned)
½ green pepper, chopped
1 large can Tomatoes, mashed but not drained
6 bay leaves
  dash paprika
½ Tsp. Worcestershire sauce
1 pkg. fine noodles cooked in salted water
  Parmesan cheese

Crumble sausage and cook slowly until brown.
  Remove from pan and drain.
Saute green pepper in 2 Tblsp. oil or sausage
  fat until glossy.
Add all other ingredients to green pepper
  and simmer for 5 minutes, stirring
  occasionally.
Put all in greased casserole. Add salt
  and pepper if necessary.
Shake Parmesan cheese generously over top.
Refrigerate.

Bake uncovered 45 minutes at 350°
  until cheese is melted.
Serve with more Parmesan cheese.

98

Crab with Eggs and Such —

The perfect luncheon dish!

5 slices white bread
2 cups Half and Half
2 cups real mayonnaise
6 hardboiled eggs, chopped
2 Tablespoons grated onion
2 Tablespoons chopped parsley
3 cans crabmeat (pink crab is best),
   drained (can use 1½ lbs. frozen King
   crab or 1½ lbs fresh crabmeat)
2 Teaspoons lemon juice
   salt and pepper to taste
½ cup freshly grated cheese
   cornflakes, crushed

Cut crusts from bread. Cut bread in
   cubes and soak in Half and Half.
   Let stand to absorb and then beat
   up this mixture with a fork.

Add mayonnaise, eggs, onion, parsley,
   crab, lemon juice, salt and pepper.
Put in casserole, sprinkling the cheese
   throughout as you do so.

Refrigerate.

When ready to bake, top with crushed
   cornflakes and bake, uncovered,
   at 350° for one hour.

Serves 6-8

Virginia Sausage

And This recipe really came from Virginia!

About 5 lbs. fresh pork, Picnic or Boston Butt
2 Tablespoons sage
1 Tablespoon salt
1 Teaspoon ground red pepper
1 Teaspoon black pepper

Cut away the bone, skin and all
   excess fat. Cut meat into 1"
   cubes.
Blend Together all the seasonings.
Mix meat well with seasonings, using
   your hands. Let stand in
   refrigerator overnight.
The next day put the meat through
   the food grinder twice, first
   using the coarse plate, then
   the medium. (If you don't
   have a medium, use coarse twice.)
   Grind slowly.

cont'd

Virginia Sausage
Cont'd

Make into patties of desired size.
Wrap patties individually in
plastic wrap and freeze. Or
put on cookie sheets, freeze,
put in a plastic bag and
pop back into freezer. I remove
desired amount of patties from
freezer and put them in the
refrigerator the night before
I plan to use them.

For best flavor you should consume
this within six weeks.

Cook patties slowly until brown.
Fresh pork should always
be well done, but do not
overcook.

If you want to try different amounts,
a good mixture for sausage is:
2/3 lean and 1/3 fat — but
we prefer it lean. You should
also adjust your seasonings
to your preference.

California Barbecue

Try This at your next cookout!

2 1/2 cans macaroni with cheese sauce (15-oz. size)
1 pkg. (9 or 10 oz.) frozen chopped spinach,
   thawed and drained
1/2 lb. freshly grated sharp cheese
1 small bunch green onions, cut up finely
1/2 tsp. oregano
1 can French-fried onions

Mix all together except french fried
   onions but save some of the
   cheese to sprinkle on top later.
Put in baking dish and refrigerate.

When ready, cover top with French
   fried onions and remaining
   cheese and bake, uncovered, in
   a 350° oven 45 to 60 minutes
   until hot through.

Serves 6

102

Stuffed Baked Potatoes

Great to keep on hand in the freezer!

4 baking potatoes
2 Tablespoons margarine, cut up
   milk — about 3 oz. more or less
1 egg, slightly beaten
1 pkg. (4 oz.) shredded cheddar cheese
2 Tablespoons chopped chives, fresh or
       freeze dried
  salt and pepper to taste
  paprika

Wash potatoes well — dry skins and rub
   them lightly with margarine or
   bacon grease. Bake at 425° for
   one hour.
Cut in half lengthwise with sharp butcher
   knife. Scoop out insides <u>carefully</u>
   and put in large mixing bowl.
Add the 2 Tablespoons margarine, milk,
   egg, and beat with electric beater
   until smooth — no lumps!
Add cheese, chives, salt and pepper. Mix well.
Heap back in shells. Put on cookie sheet.
Sprinkle with paprika. Freeze thoroughly.
   Put in plastic bag.
When ready, thaw, and bake at 350°
   for 25 minutes.

Serves 8

103

Tomato Side Dish

Your friends will ask, "How did you make This?"

2 large cans solid pack Tomatoes
8 whole cloves
8 whole peppercorns
1 bay leaf (at least 1 inch long)
    salt
1/2 yellow onion, chopped
3/4 cup brown sugar
3 or 4 slices white bread pulled into
    dime size pieces.
2 Tblsp. butter

Put cloves, peppercorns, and bay leaf
    in cheesecloth bag.
Cook Tomatoes, undrained, cheesecloth bag,
    and a dash of salt on top of stove
    very slowly 30 minutes. Stir occasionally.
Add onion, sugar, bread, and butter.
Place in greased baking dish.

When ready to bake, remove cheesecloth
    bag and contents and bake at 400°
    1 hour.

Serves 6

Fried Rice

This really special casserole can be made
the main dish by adding shrimp, chicken,
ham or turkey.

2 Tblsp. salad oil
1 bunch green onion, chopped. (Include
    some of the green tops.)
1 generous cup chopped celery
2 cups cooked rice
    salt to taste
2 Tblsp. soy sauce (or 3 if you prefer)
    slivered almonds, browned in butter

Sauté onions and celery in oil, but
    do not brown
Add rice, a bit of salt, and soy sauce
Mix and place in casserole.

When ready to bake, place in 350°
    oven for about 30 minutes — or
    until hot through.
Toss almonds on top just before
    serving.

Serves 4

Noodles and Mushrooms

This is delicious with ham or any roast.

1 white onion
1 green pepper
½ cup salad oil
½ can cream style corn
1 can Tomato soup
1 box medium wide noodles
1 small can chopped or sliced ripe olives
1 small can mushrooms, drained
  grated cheese

Dice pepper and onions and fry slowly in
  oil until glossy.
Boil noodles 9 minutes.
Mix all ingredients Together (except cheese)
  and place in casserole. Refrigerate.

When ready To bake, cover Top with
  grated cheese. Place casserole in pan
  containing a small amount of warm
  water and bake at 350° for 1 hour.

If you wish To use it as a main dish,
  brown 1 pound of ground round or
  chuck and add To casserole.

Green Rice

Perfect for a luncheon with salad.

3 cups cooked white rice
2 1/2 cups milk
2 cups grated sharp cheese
2 eggs, beaten
2 Tsp. olive oil - or salad oil
1 cup chopped parsley
4 green onions, chopped fine
1 large Tsp. Worcestershire sauce

Mix all, season well with salt
and pepper, and place in
greased casserole.

When ready To bake, place in
350° oven for 45 minutes.

Serves 6

107

Spinach

This way you will like your spinach!

2 pkgs. frozen chopped spinach (10 oz. each)
1/2 pint commercial sour cream
1 envelope dehydrated onion soup (1 1/2 oz.)
  dash of Tabasco
  salt and pepper (go easy on the salt)
1/4 cup chopped nuts — any kind

Cook spinach as directed on package,
  using minimum cooking time.
  Drain well.
Mix spinach, sour cream, soup mix,
  Tabasco, salt and pepper
Refrigerate.
When ready to bake, place in 350°
  oven, uncovered, for 20 minutes.
Sprinkle nuts on top and bake
  15 minutes more.

Serves 4 —

Green and Yellow Rice

This is supposed to serve 8 but it won't because your guests will consume quantities!

3 cups boiled rice - use any kind - I use precooked.

1/4 cup butter or margarine

4 beaten eggs

1 lb. grated sharp cheddar cheese - grate it at home - don't buy it already grated!

1 cup milk

1 pkg. frozen, chopped spinach - cooked and drained

1 Tblsp. chopped onion

1 Tblsp. Worcestershire Sauce

1/2 Teasp. each marjoram, thyme, rosemary, and salt.

Boil rice to obtain the 3 cups.

Melt butter and add to rice - unless you added it as with precooked rice.

Beat eggs and grate cheese.

Add milk to eggs - then add cheese - then spinach - and mix well, but gently. Add onion, Worcestershire, and seasonings. Set aside after placing in 2-qt casserole.

When ready, set casserole, uncovered, in pan of warm water and bake at 350° for 45 minutes. Serves 6?

Colorful Carrots

In my estimation this is the perfect
side dish for a barbecue!

1 pkg. fresh carrots ~ or about 1½ lbs.
1 green pepper
1 yellow onion
1 can (10¾ oz.) tomato soup
1 cup sugar
⅓ cup salad oil
¾ cup vinegar
1 tablespoon salt
1 tablespoon coarse or freshly ground pepper

Peel carrots and slice lengthwise into slim
strips about 4" long. Boil until
tender but still crisp (10-15 minutes.)
Drain.
Cut away seeds and white membrane from
inside green pepper, and cut it into
slim strips.
Peel and thinly slice onion and separate into rings.
Lay all this in oblong dish (8" x 12" x 1½".)
Bring remaining ingredients to a boil, stir
well, and while hot, pour over vegetables.
Refrigerate when cool.
It's delicious ~ and will keep, refrigerated,
for several days.
Serve it cold ~ To 8

Baked Zucchini

A real favorite!

3 lbs. zucchini
1 yellow onion
   parsley
3 or 4 Tablespoons biscuit or pancake
   flour
   salt and pepper to taste
3 eggs, beaten
   grated cheese
   butter
   paprika

Cut off the tip ends of zucchini and
   wash but do not peel.
Grate or chop fine the zucchini, onion,
   and parsley.
Add the flour, salt, pepper and eggs, and
   stir all.
Butter a flat baking dish (about 9"x13")
   and add the zucchini mixture.
Sprinkle with cheese.
Dot with butter.
Sprinkle with paprika.
Set aside.
When ready, bake uncovered at 350°
   for 40 minutes. If deep casserole
   is used, layer the zucchini,
   cheese, butter and paprika and
   increase the baking time.

Serves 4-6

How To Bake Rice
Tender and buttery!

1 cup raw white rice
1 cube (4 oz.) butter or margarine,
    cut into 8 slices
10 oz. water (from your faucet)
10 oz. boiling water
    salt to taste

Put all in greased 1½-qt. baking
    dish. Stir.
Cover and bake at 350° for one hour.
    Do not stir while baking, but
    do stir up from bottom before
    serving.
If you want to do a bit ahead, do
    not add waters until ready
    to bake

Serves 6 —

112

Stuffed Pimientos
A tasty, colorful side dish!

1 pkg. (3 oz.) cream cheese
1 pkg. (4 oz.) shredded cheddar cheese
2/3 cup dry seasoned poultry stuffing -
    crushed with rolling pin - measure
    after crushing.

2 eggs, beaten
1 heaping teaspoon wet mustard
1/2 teaspoon salt
1/4 teaspoon pepper
1/4 teaspoon Tabasco
2 cans (4 oz. each) whole pimientos

Whip cream cheese with a fork
    until smooth.
Add all but pimientos and mix well
Drain pimientos and stuff with
    this filling.
Grease a flat baking dish (I use
    6½" x 10½") and lay pimientos
    side by side.
Cover with sauce on following page.

Sauce for Pimientos

See preceding page

¼ lb. fresh mushrooms
1 can (10¾ oz.) cream of celery soup
1 can (10¾ oz.) cream of mushroom soup
5 strips bacon

Chop mushrooms very fine.

Mix soup (undiluted) together and stir
in mushrooms. Pour over
pimientos Refrigerate.

Fry bacon until crisp. Drain, crumble,
and put in small covered jar.

When ready, sprinkle bacon over
pimientos and bake, uncovered,
at 350° for 45 minutes.

There is plenty of filling for 8 pimientos,
but sometimes there are 3 and sometimes 4 pimientos in one can. So if
you plan to serve 8, bear this in mind

Brown Rice Deluxe

And you'll like it! A West Coast recipe.

1 cup quick cooking brown rice
1 can (3½ oz.) french fried onions
2 cans Mushroom Soup
¼ cup stuffed green olives, sliced
1 can (2 oz.) mushroom stems and pieces
½ cup milk
¼ Teasp. pepper
¼ cup freshly grated Parmesan or
   cheddar cheese

Cook brown rice according to directions on box.
   Drain and place in 2-QT. casserole.
Add the onions, mushrooms, and olives - but
   save the juice from the mushrooms.
   Mix all gently.
In another bowl put the soup, milk,
   pepper, and juice from mushrooms.
   Set all aside.

When ready to bake, pour the mushroom
   soup mixture into rice mixture
   and mix all gently. Bake, uncovered,
   at 350° for 30 minutes. Then
   sprinkle cheese over the top. Bake
   for 10 more minutes.

Serves 6

Norfolk Noodles

Mighty Tasty!

12 oz. wide noodles
1 cup fresh parsley, chopped
1 pt. carton cottage cheese - large curd
1 pt. carton commercial sour cream
1 Tblsp. Worcestershire sauce
   dash Tobasco
1 bunch green onions, chopped. Be sure
   to use some of the onion tops.
½ cup grated sharp cheese
½ teasp. paprika

Boil noodles according to directions on
   the package. Drain.
While noodles are still hot, mix in all
   the remaining ingredients except
   cheese and paprika.
Place in a baking dish, preferably shallow.
Refrigerate.
When ready to bake, top with cheese
   and paprika. Place in 350° oven,
   uncovered, for 40 minutes or
   until hot through and cheese is
   melted.
   Serves 8

116

Green Bean Casserole

Specially good with barbecued chicken!

1/2 cup minced onion
2 Tablespoons butter
1 garlic clove, crushed
1 Tablespoon flour
1/2 pint sour cream
2 pkgs. (9 oz. each) green beans – French
    Style (frozen)
    RITZ CRACKER crumbs

Sauté onion in butter along with
    garlic clove.
Stir in the flour.
Slowly add the sour cream, stirring
    constantly until hot.
Partially cook the green beans.
Mix sauce with green beans and
    place in casserole.
Refrigerate.
When ready to bake, cover with
    the crumbs and bake in a
    350° oven for 40 minutes.

Serves 4 to 6

117

White Rice Browned

Our bachelor friend makes a whole meal out of this!

½ cup butter or margarine
2 cups raw white rice
2¼ Tsp. salt
¼ Tsp. pepper
2 cans beef consommé
2 cups water
½ cup chopped, blanched almonds (I prepare these ahead - or buy them canned.)

Melt butter in large frying pan
Add rice
Cook over very slow fire, stirring often, until rice is golden brown.
Place in 2-qt. casserole.
Sprinkle on seasonings.

When ready to bake, add consommé, water, and nuts. Mix gently.
Cover and bake at 300° for 1 hour and 15 minutes. Do not stir.

Serves 10

Potato Casserole

A delicious potato dish using <u>canned</u> potatoes!

2 cans small white potatoes
parsley, chopped
pepper
Dill seed
Oregano
1 can mushroom soup
1 soup can of milk
garlic powder
paprika

Drain potatoes and place in baking dish.
Sprinkle generously with parsley.
Season with pepper.
Sprinkle with a pinch of dill seed.
Sprinkle with 2 pinches oregano, crumbled.
Dilute 1 can mushroom soup with 1 can milk.
Stir 1/8 Tsp. garlic powder into soup.
Pour this over potatoes.
Sprinkle paprika over top.

When ready to bake, place baking dish
in 350° oven, covered, until hot—
about 45 minutes.

Serves 4-6

119

Mushrooms and Rice

I could eat this every night!

2 2/3 cups precooked rice
6 Tblsp. salad oil
2 small cans mushrooms, drained
    green onions, chopped
2 cans beef consommé, undiluted
2 Tblsp. soya sauce
1/2 Tsp. salt

Mix and bake, covered, at 350° until
    water is absorbed, no more than
    30-45 minutes. Do not stir.

To prepare in advance, place dry
    ingredients in casserole and
    add liquids just before baking.

Serves 6

120

For Fish

Great little side dish with any fish!

Cucumber.
Cider vinegar
Cold water.
Salt, if desired

Wash and slice cucumber, but do not
     peel. Lay in a flat-ish dish.
Mix together 1/3 vinegar to 2/3 water
     and pour over cucumber slices.
     Make enough to just cover slices.
Sprinkle on a little salt if you wish.
Marinate in refrigerator at least an hour.
Drain before serving.

For Beef

Is the same as above, but use
     Bermuda (red) onions instead
     of cucumber — and do peel
     the onions.

121

Pear Side Dish

So simple ~ delicious with pork!

Canned pears ~ whatever size you need
Chutney

Place pear halves in flat baking
   dish.

Pour in enough juice from can to
   cover bottom of dish about 1/4".

Fill each center with chutney.

When ready, bake at 350°, uncovered,
   for 20-25 minutes until hot
   through.

Molded Salad

Perfect with clam dish on p. 97

1 pkg. lemon jello (3 oz.)
1 1/2 Tblsp. vinegar
1/2 cup real mayonnaise
1/4 tsp. salt
1/3 cup chopped celery
1 Tblsp. minced onion
1 cup chopped frozen spinach, thawed
      and well drained
3/4 cup cottage cheese

Dissolve jello in 3/4 cup boiling water.
Add one cup cold water.
Add vinegar, mayonnaise and salt.
Put in freezer tray and chill until
      firm 1 inch around sides of tray.
Turn into bowl and beat until fluffy.
Add celery, onion, spinach and cottage
      cheese.
Place in 1-qt. mold and chill in
      refrigerator until firm.
Best To do a day ahead — due to
      chilling twice.

Serves 4-6

123

Coronado Salad Ring

So delicious and complete that it needs
no dressing.

1 pkg. lime jello (3 oz.)
1 pkg. lemon jello (3 oz.)
2 cups hot water
10 oz. small curd creamed cottage cheese
1 #2 can crushed pineapple, well drained
2/3 cup chopped walnuts
8 oz. whipping cream, not whipped
1 cup mayonnaise
1 Tblsp. prepared horseradish (wet type)

Dissolve the jellos in the hot water.
Add remaining ingredients in the
        order given.
Place in wet ring mold and refrigerate
        until firm.
When ready to serve, unmold onto
        a platter. Fill center with
        fresh strawberries.

Serves 8 —

124

Mixed Bean Salad

Ideal for a barbecue. A wonderfully
  "fool-proof" recipe!

1 can green beans - No. 303 size (2 cups)
1 can wax beans - same size
1 can red kidney beans - same size
½ cup chopped green pepper
¾ cup sugar
⅔ cup cider vinegar
⅓ cup salad oil
1 Teasp. pepper
1 Teasp. salt

Drain canned beans well.
Add chopped green pepper to beans.
Combine remaining ingredients and
    mix well.
Now mix all together and let stand,
    refrigerated, for 24 hours.
Drain off excess liquid before serving.

Serves 6 generously.

My Favorite French Dressing

2 cups olive or salad oil
1/2 cup red wine vinegar, garlic flavor
2 Tsp. salt
2 Tsp. freshly ground pepper
2 Tsp. wet mustard
2 Tsp. Worcestershire Sauce

Beat all with an egg beater and store in
refrigerator in covered container.

Always shake well before using.

For Roquefort or Bleu cheese dressing,
just add desired amount of
crumbled cheeses and beat along
with rest of ingredients.

Add dressing to salad just before
serving.

Parsley Dressing for Fresh Tomatoes

Entirely different - and can be made days ahead.

2 cups fresh parsley
1/2 cup chopped chives
1 cup sweet pickles, drained
2 cloves garlic
salt and pepper to suit

Cut the chives very fine (I use scissors)

Then put all the above ingredients through the food grinder twice. Use the small blade. Save any juice that may escape.

Then add:
     1/2 cup olive oil
     1/2 cup red wine vinegar
     1/4 cup tarragon vinegar
          The juice from grinding

Mix all well and keep at room temperature for 24 hours in a covered jar. Then refrigerate.

Serve ice cold on platter of chilled, peeled, sliced tomatoes.

Will keep, refrigerated, covered, for 2 weeks.

127

Pineapple - Cheese Salad Ring

½ pound cottage cheese
1 cup whipped cream
1 Tblsp. gelatine
½ cup water
2½ cups grated pineapple, drained
2 Tblsp. mayonnaise
½ Tsp. salt.

Rub cottage cheese through a
sieve. Add salt.
Soak gelatine in cold water and
dissolve over hot water.
Add cheese, mix well.
Add mayonnaise, pineapple, and cream.
Chill in ring until firm.

When ready, unmold and serve with
a dressing of mayonnaise plus a
little lemon juice and a little
whipped cream. Use fresh fruit in
center of ring.

128

Spinach Salad

Different! And so healthy!

2 cellophane pkgs. fresh spinach (or 1¼ lbs.)
   Salad oil
   lemon juice

Wash spinach - shake gently to dry - cut
   off all stems.
Then, using scissors, cut spinach leaves in
   one-inch-wide pieces.
Sprinkle a little oil on leaves - then a
   little lemon juice. Barely dampen the
   leaves - do not saturate!
Refrigerate.

Serve with a side dish of:

Chili Dressing

  1 cup mayonnaise
  ¼ cup chili sauce
    juice of 1 lemon
    minced green onion to taste.
  Mix well and chill until ready to serve.

Serves 6 to 8

129

Vermicelli Salad
Really ideal for the hot summertime!

1   12-oz. pkg. vermicelli
5   hard-boiled eggs, chopped
5   stalks of celery, chopped
6   good-sized sweet pickles, chopped
1/4 small yellow onion, chopped fine
    salt to taste
1 1/2 cups real mayonnaise
2   cans shrimp or crab (4 1/2-oz. size)
        drained, washed gently, and chilled
    Paprika

Break vermicelli in half and boil as
    directed on the package. Drain
    thoroughly in colander and run
    under cold water well to prevent
    sticking.
When vermicelli is cool, add next 6
    ingredients and mix well. Refrigerate.
Just before serving, add shrimp or
    crab and toss lightly.
Sprinkle with paprika and serve to
    10 or 12 happy guests!

130

Dressing for Coleslaw

1/3 cup real mayonnaise
3 Tblsp. milk
1 or 2 Tblsp. pickle juice - depending
    on how tart you like it. (Use
    juice from sweet pickles, not dill.)
Minced green onion or green onion tops

Mix mayonnaise and milk
Stir in pickle juice.
Add onions.
Chill.

When ready to serve, add to 1
    pkg. fresh coleslaw or amount
    to serve 4. Toss well.

131

Potato Salad

4 cups diced, boiled potatoes
1 cup diced cucumber
3 Tblsp. minced onion
1 1/2 Tsp. salt
1/2 Tsp. pepper
3 hard-boiled eggs, diced

Mix the above and toss with the
following dressing:

Dressing

1 1/2 cups sour cream (commercial)
1/2 cup mayonnaise
1/4 cup vinegar
3/4 Tsp. celery seed
1 Tsp. wet mustard

Chill salad until ready to serve.

Serves 6 amply

Lewiston Salad Dressing

My mother's favorite! Good on any
kind of salad.

Juice of one large lemon, strained
6 Tblsp. olive oil (no substitute)
1 Teasp. salt
½ Teasp. pepper
½ clove garlic - if desired.

Mix in the order given and stir well.
Make it several hours ahead of time
    and let stand at room temperature.
When ready to serve, remove the
    garlic and again stir the
    dressing well.

For a salad serving 4 persons.

133

Cranberry Salad Mold

2 cans jellied cranberry sauce
2 envelopes gelatine
1/2 cup cold water
1/2 Tsp. salt
2/3 cup chopped walnuts
2/3 cup diced apples
1/2 cup chopped celery

Crush sauce with a fork.
Put gelatine in water - let stand 2 minutes. (Do this in a small, flat bowl.) Place dish in pan of boiling water after gelatine is absorbed! Let stand until dissolved. Stir a bit.
Add gelatine to cranberry sauce and stir until smooth. Place in refrigerator for 1 or 2 hours until partially jelled.
Add remaining ingredients and pour into mold. Chill until firm.

Unmold when ready and pass mayonnaise when serving. Add a little red wine vinegar to mayonnaise if you want it more tart.

If made a day ahead, keep in refrigerator covered with aluminum foil.

134

Cream Dressing for Salads

1 pt. real mayonnaise
2 Tblsp. (generous) anchovy paste
3 Tblsp. Tarragon or red wine vinegar
1 Tblsp. scraped onion
1 small clove garlic, minced
6 filets of anchovy, chopped
      (if you omit this, double the paste.)
1 Tblsp. chopped, fresh parsley
1 Tblsp. chives or green onion tops, cut fine

Mix vinegar with mayonnaise.
Add other ingredients. Mix well.
Chill.

I serve this on a salad of only
      romaine lettuce.

If you yearn for a Roquefort cream
      dressing, just grate desired
      amount of Roquefort cheese
      into dressing and mix well.
      Omit all anchovy.
This is best made a day or so ahead.

Be sure to add all salad dressings
      just before serving - and toss well.

135

Pear Ring Mold

1 pkg. lime jello
canned pear halves
2 pkgs. cream cheese

Make lime jello according to directions on pkg.
Take half of it and pour over some canned
  pears in quart ring mold. Place in refrigerator to "set" a little. (1 or 2 hours)
Take other half of jello and add the cream
  cheese which has been put through a sieve.
Let this stand at room temperature until
  the first mixture has "set" partially.
Then pour jello-cheese mixture over jello-
  pear mixture and return mold to
  refrigerator to completely jell.

This can be served with 2 or 3 cups fresh
  grapes in center. Mix grapes into following sauce:

     2 egg yolks, well beaten
     1 Tblsp. sugar
     a little salt
     2 Tblsp. Tarragon vinegar
  Cook above in double boiler very carefully until pretty thick. Chill, and
  when cold, add 1/2 pt. or less of
  whipped cream. Add grapes.
For the whole mold serve a dressing of
  mayonnaise with a little salad oil
  and lemon juice to taste added.

Blender Blue Cheese Dressing

Good, too, as a dip for raw vegetables!

½ pint real mayonnaise
1 tablespoon lemon juice
½ pint sour cream
1 small jar (5 oz.) blue cheese spread
1 clove garlic, minced

Put in blender in order given
    and mix until fluffy —
    about 2 minutes.

137

Molded Beet Salad

Popular with men, particularly, since it is not sweet.

1 can (1 lb.) shoestring beets
1 pkg. (3 oz.) lemon-flavored gelatine
1/4 cup sugar
1/4 cup vinegar
1 Tablespoon prepared horseradish

Drain beets but save juice.
   Measure juice and add enough water to make 1 1/2 cups liquid.
Bring liquid to a boil. Remove from heat.
To the liquid add the lemon gelatine, sugar, vinegar, and horseradish. Stir until gelatine and sugar are dissolved.
Add beets.
Pour into mold — or dish — and place in refrigerator until firm.
Serve with real mayonnaise to which you have added some red wine vinegar to taste.

Serves 6

138

Dressing for Fruit Salad

½ cup sugar
1 Teaspoon salt
1 Teaspoon dry mustard
1 Teaspoon celery seed
1 Teaspoon paprika
1 Teaspoon onion, finely grated
1 cup olive oil
¼ cup white vinegar (or you can
    use cider vinegar as second choice)

Mix dry ingredients and add onion.
Then add oil and vinegar a little
    bit at a Time – stirring constantly.
    (I use a beater)

Keep in refrigerator.

Try 2 or 3 Tablespoons of This
    over drained fresh grapefruit
    segments.

Vegetable Mold

One of my favorite party molds!

1 1/4 cup celery, chopped
1 yellow onion, chopped
1/2 large green pepper, chopped. (First remove
    seeds and membranes inside.)
1 cucumber, chopped. (Remove Tips but don't peel.)
1 pkg. (8 oz.) cream cheese, softened
1 can (10 3/4 oz.) tomato soup, undiluted
1/4 cup lemon juice
3/4 cup water
2 pkgs. (3 oz each) lemon jello. Or one 6-oz. pkg.
1 cup real mayonnaise
1/2 cup chopped walnuts
    parsley for top

Put celery, onion, pepper and cucumber
    through food grinder using medium blade.
    Drain in colander or large strainer.
Whip cheese with fork, add soup, and mix well.
Bring lemon juice and water to a boil. Add
    jello and stir until dissolved.
Pour cheese-soup mixture into jello. Add
    vegetables and mayonnaise. Beat all
    with egg beater. Fold in nuts.
Grease a flat 2-qt. dish with salad oil and
    pour all into dish. Refrigerate overnight
    until firm.
Sprinkle with parsley; cut in squares to serve
    on lettuce. You can mix a little red wine
    vinegar with mayonnaise and put a dab
    on top of each square.
Serves 10 easily.

140

Lazy Salad Sandwich

Try this for your next luncheon. It's fun to make - fun for your guests - and a real conversation piece!

Place about 3 lettuce leaves (preferably red lettuce, if you can get it) on a dinner-sized plate.

Put in the center a well-flavored egg sandwich (use chopped pickle, mayonnaise, salt and pepper) and cut off the crusts but do not cut it in half. Also, boil an extra egg and save it, chopped, for later.

On the sandwich place 1 large or 2 smaller slices of peeled tomato.

On top of this put crab or shrimp.

Place a couple of olives and a pickled beet on the side.

Then have a huge bowl of really rich Thousand Island type dressing. (To 1 cup of real mayonnaise I add 2 heaping Tblsp. chili sauce, 1 Tblsp. finely chopped green pepper, 1 Tblsp. chopped green onion and the chopped egg you saved.) Your guests cover their sandwich with the dressing.

You may serve potato chips if you like, but no bread is necessary. All is on one plate.

This may all be prepared in advance and assembled at the last minute.

141

Weekend Soups

Onion and Cheese:

 1 can or pkg. onion soup
 1 slice American cheese - per person
 1 slice French bread - per person

Make soup according to directions
In each bowl put one slice toasted bread,
  lightly buttered.
Top the toast with a slice of cheese.
Over all this pour the hot soup.

Corn:

 1 can (17 oz.) cream style corn
 1 can (10½ oz.) chicken and rice soup
 1 pint Half and Half
 salt to taste
 paprika

Whir soups in blender.
Add Half and Half, salt, and heat slowly,
  stirring often. Do not boil.
Sprinkle paprika on each bowl before serving.

Mystery Soup: (You can't guess contents!.)

 1 can (10½ oz.) cream of Asparagus soup, undiluted
 1 cup milk (nonfat is OK)
 ¼ teaspoon Tabasco - ½ teaspoon celery salt
 1 cup commercial sour cream
 1 thin slice of onion, minced
  minced chives

Mix all but chives in blender. Refrigerate.
Reheat, stirring, and serve in mugs with
  chives on top.

142

Diet Soup

We love this!

1 can (10¾ oz.) cream of chicken soup
¼ cup juice from canned mushrooms
1 cup nonfat milk
½ cup water
½ teaspoon curry powder
1 Tablespoon green onion tops

Heat all slowly, stirring until
    smooth.
Or make ahead, refrigerate, and
    reheat later.

Makes 3 8-oz. servings ——

Christmas Cookies

An annual affair at our house. Really glamorous cookies!

6 cups sifted flour
1 Teasp. salt
2 cups butter (1 lb.) no substitute!
2 cups granulated sugar
4 unbeaten eggs
2 Teasp. vanilla extract

Sift flour and salt together.

Cream butter until soft. Gradually add sugar, creaming after each addition until it is light and fluffy.

Add eggs and vanilla to butter-sugar mixture and mix well. (May become lumpy but keep mixing until lumps are small.)

Add flour-salt mixture a little at a time and mix well.

Cover bowl and refrigerate at least 5 hours.

Roll out dough to ⅛ inch thickness. Use a small portion of dough at a time and be sure to flour your board, rolling pin, and cutters often or dough will stick to board.

Cut out shapes with cookie cutters, dipping them in flour each time.

(cont'd)

Christmas Cookies (cont'd)

Place on ungreased cookie sheet and bake at 375° for about 10 minutes or until light brown around the edges.

When cool, frost as described below.

We use as cutters a star, a bell, a tree, and a gingerbread boy who makes a fine Santa.

Makes 70 to 90 cookies, depending on which cutters you choose.

Frosting for Christmas Cookies

4 egg whites
1/2 teasp. cream of tartar
1/2 teasp. vanilla
5 cups sifted confectioners sugar
candy cake decorations and food coloring

Now comes the fun!

Beat egg whites with cream of tartar and vanilla until foamy.
Gradually beat in the sifted powdered sugar until frosting stands in firm peaks.
Now gather the family around the table.
Divide the frosting among 5 custard or teacups. Tint 4 of the cups with food coloring — red, blue, green, and yellow. If necessary use more than 1 bottle of coloring each because you want bright colors! The 5th cup will be white.

145

Frosting for Christmas Cookies (Cont'd)

Place an individual butter spreader or small
  knife in each cup.
Have several bottles of cake decorations nearby.

Now you are ready! Give each cookie a
  complete "color job". Green Christmas
  Trees then have garlands of all colors -
  and ornaments of cake decorations. Each
  star is gaily colored - perhaps striped -
  and maybe has multi-colored tips. Dots
  and designs of all kinds grace your bells.
  Santa is complete with white beard and
  belt, blue eyes, and buttons down the front.
  My husband delights our children with
  his gingerbread boy transformed into
  a sailor in blues proudly wearing his
  campaign ribbons!

These are really gay. Just be sure you
  give each cookie a complete coating.
  None of the cookie itself should show -
    just the decorative frosting. Have
    fun - and let your imagination have
    a field day!

(If frosting hardens, add a few drops of
  hot water.)

Apple Dessert

Ideal for a cold winter day!

2 cans (about 1 lb., 5 oz. each) Apple
    Pie Filling — sometimes called
    "Apples for Pies."
2 cups spice cake mix (dry)
1 pkg. (2 7/8 oz.) slivered almonds
4 oz. (1 cube) butter, melted

Spread the apple filling on the bottom
    of a flat, greased, baking dish. I use
    a 2-qt. size which is 12" x 7½" x 2".
45 minutes before you want to serve
    it, sprinkle the cake mix on top of
    the apples. Then scatter on the
    almonds. Drizzle the butter over all.
Bake in a 375° oven for 40 minutes.

Serve warm - with cream.

Serves 8 —

Chocolate-Mint Angel Cake

Delicious, pretty to see, and made a
  day ahead!

1 Angel cake (about 10" size)
1 Qt. whipping cream
1 cup granulated sugar
4 heaping Tblsp. cocoa
  dash of salt
1 Tsp. Peppermint Extract
  Bitter chocolate

When cake is cool, slice crosswise
  in 4 layers. Set aside while
  you make the following filling.

Mix together the cream, sugar, cocoa,
  salt, and extract. Put in
  refrigerator for 1 hour. Then
  whip to proper consistency for
  icing.

Now put the cake back together
  again, icing each layer as you
  go. Ice sides. Grate bitter
  chocolate on the top of iced
  cake. You may add some slivered
  almonds (which you have browned
  in butter) for decoration.

Make the day before and refrigerate
  overnight.

Serves 10 generously and 12 easily.

148

Whiskey Ice Box Cake

A delectable dessert for 12.

2 envelopes gelatine
½ cup cold water
½ cup boiling water
6 eggs, separated
7 or 8 Tblsp. whiskey
1 cup sugar
1 Teasp. lemon juice
1 pt. whipping cream
3 pkgs. ladyfingers, split

Soak gelatine in cold water. Then add
    boiling water and dissolve.
Beat egg yolks until thick.
Add whiskey very slowly.
Beat in the sugar.
Add lemon juice.
Stir in gelatine and chill a short time.
Whip cream and fold it in.
Beat egg whites and fold in.
Line sides and bottom of a springform
    pan (about 12") with split ladyfingers.
Pour the mixture in slowly. When about
    half way, put in a layer of ladyfingers.
Then, when filled, place a layer of ladyfingers
    on top in a design.
Chill overnight in the refrigerator.

Over and Over Again Bars

The name of this recipe tells you
how often you will use it!!

1 cube (4 oz.) butter or margarine
1 cup Graham Cracker crumbs
    (roll with rolling pin - or buy in a
    package)
1 package (6 oz.) semi-sweet choco-
    late bits
1 cup flaked coconut
1 cup Grapenuts (cereal)
1 can (14 oz.) Condensed Milk

In a 325° oven, melt the butter or
    margarine in a 9" x 13" baking
    dish or pan. (Don't let it burn!!)
Remove from the oven and sprinkle
    evenly over the butter or
    margarine in this order:
        The Graham Cracker crumbs
        The chocolate bits
        The flaked coconut
        The Grapenuts
Drizzle the can of milk over all.
Bake at 325° (you may like them
    crispier by using 350°) for 30
    minutes. Cool in dish. Cut
    into squares or bars.
These freeze well.

150

Christmas Cookies II

Similar to fruit cake, but I like them better!

1 Teaspoon soda
1/4 cup hot water
2 cups flour
2/3 cup butter
1 cup sugar
2 eggs
1 lb. pecans, chopped
1 lb. pineapple and 1 lb. cherries (the kind you use in fruit cake) both chopped
1 lb. dates, chopped
1 Teaspoon powdered cloves
1 Teaspoon cinnamon
1/2 cup whiskey

Dissolve soda in water and cool.

Brown flour in heavy skillet over very low heat, stirring constantly.

Mix flour with soda-water mixture.

Cream butter with sugar and add to above.

Slightly beat the eggs and add.

Add remaining ingredients and mix gently.

Drop by teaspoons on well-greased and floured cookie sheet.

Bake at 350° until brown. Watch carefully as it does not take long — about 12 minutes.

Store in cans — or as you would fruit cake.

These may be hard to take off cookie sheet but they will soften in the can. Can add a piece of cut apple to the can.

Makes about 70 cookies —

151

Bremerton Bourbon Balls

No-cook cookies!

2½ cups crushed vanilla wafers
   (Most of a 12 oz. pkg.)
2 Tblsp. cocoa
1 cup confectioners sugar (sift before
   measuring.)
1 cup chopped walnuts
3 Tblsp. corn syrup or honey
¼ cup bourbon or brandy or rum
   confectioners sugar for topping

Mix well The crumbs, cocoa, The
   1 cup sugar, and The nuts.
Add The corn syrup and liquor. Mix
   all very Thoroughly.
Form into one-inch balls, Then roll
   in confectioners sugar. That's
   all!

Note: Keep in a covered Tin. These
   are even better The second day.

Makes 3 To 3½ dozen cookies.

152

Cracker Pie

Be sure to make this!

3 egg whites
1 cup sugar
1 Teasp. baking powder
1/2 Teasp. vanilla
3/4 cup chopped nuts (walnuts or pecans)
1 cup cracker crumbs (RITZ CRACKERS or
        WAVERLY WAFERS)
Ice cream (vanilla)

Beat egg whites until stiff.
Add sugar, baking powder, and vanilla.
    Mix each in well.
Fold in nuts.
Add cracker crumbs (crumbs are easily
    obtained by using a rolling pin.)
Mix all carefully and pour into
    well-greased 8" pie plate.
Bake 30 minutes at 350°. Let cool in
    its plate but outside oven.
Cut in wedges, Top with ice cream,
    and serve to 6 happy
        dessert lovers!
Pie freezes well, too.

153

Butterscotch Toffee Heavenly Delight

As good as it sounds!

1 1/2 cups whipping cream
1 can (5 1/2 oz.) butterscotch syrup (Topping)
1/2 teasp. vanilla extract
1 unfrosted angel cake (9 1/2")
3/4 lb. English Toffee, crushed (put through food grinder using largest blade.)

Whip cream until it starts to thicken.
Add butterscotch syrup and vanilla slowly and continue beating until thick.
Cut cake into 3 layers - horizontally.
Spread the butterscotch mixture on the layers and sprinkle each generously with crushed Toffee.
Put cake back together again and frost the top and sides with butterscotch mixture and sprinkle them, too, with Toffee.
Place cake in the refrigerator and chill for a minimum of 6 hours.

Serves 12

154

Washington Cookies

Our favorites!

1 1/2 cups flour
1 Tsp. soda
1 Tsp. salt
1 cup margarine
3/4 cup brown sugar
3/4 cup granulated sugar

2 eggs
1 Tsp. vanilla
1 cup chopped walnuts
2 cups rolled oats
1 pkg. chocolate bits — 6 oz.

Sift flour, measure and sift again with soda and salt.

Cream margarine with brown and white sugar.

Beat eggs into margarine-sugar mixture.

Add vanilla and mix well.

Stir in dry ingredients.

Add nuts, oats, and bits and mix all thoroughly.

Drop on greased cookie sheet (about 1 Tblsp. batter for each cookie) and bake 10-12 minutes at 350° until light brown.

Makes about 6 dozen delicious cookies

Crème Chocolate

Fun to serve in after-dinner coffee cups!

1 pkg. chocolate bits
4 Tblsp. cold water
5 eggs, separated
whipped cream

Put chocolate bits in pan with the cold water. Stir over low heat, with wooden spoon, until well blended.

Remove from the fire and slowly stir in the 5 egg yolks which have been well beaten. Mix well.

Fold in the 5 stiffly beaten whites. Continue until all is well blended.

Pour into after-dinner coffee cups and store in refrigerator at least 5 hours - preferably overnight.

Serve in cups with a bit of whipped cream - unsweetened, as this is a very rich dessert.

Fills 10 cups.

156

Lemon Ice Cream

So light, delicate, and refreshing!

1 cup granulated sugar
7 Tblsp. fresh lemon juice (about 4 lemons)
2 cups Half and Half

Mix together the sugar and lemon juice.
Stir it carefully into the Half and Half.
Pour into freezer tray in top of your
    refrigerator.
Stir gently while it is freezing. I do this
    after 40 minutes and after 40 minutes
    more, using a fork to crush any lumps.
Finish freezing. Remove from freezer about
    10 minutes before serving - less in hot
    climate.
                        Serves 5

Orange Ice Cream

Easy - and with a different flavor!

2 pints vanilla ice cream - softened, not melted.
2 small cans frozen orange juice, undiluted
2 generous ounces Grand Marnier liqueur

Soften ice cream and thaw orange juice.
Mix all together well and put in freezer tray.
Freeze it - tho' it won't get really hard.
Serve in sherbets with a cookie or slice
    of cake.
                        Serves 8

157

Lazy-Dazy Cake

A favorite of young and old alike!

1 pkg. (18½ oz.) lemon cake mix
1 pkg. (3½ oz.) instant vanilla pudding
¾ cup real mayonnaise
¾ cup water
4 whole eggs
    powdered sugar

Preheat oven to 350° and line a
    7½" x 12" x 2" baking dish with
    brown paper
Put first four ingredients in large
    mixing bowl and mix with
    electric beater at low speed
    until smooth.
Add eggs, one at a time, beating a
    minimum of one minute at
    medium speed after each addition.
Pour batter into lined dish and bake at
    350° for 50 minutes. Cool in dish
    for 15 minutes and remove.
When completely cool, sift sugar on top
    or serve "as is" with fresh fruit.
If you freeze it, thaw before adding sugar.
Try different flavors of cake and pudding mixes.

Right size dish is important.

158

Pasadena Peach Delight

The perfect dessert for a hot summer
  evening! And particularly good after seafood.

1 pkg. ladyfingers (about 10)
  Peach Brandy
2 pkgs. frozen sliced peaches (semi-thawed)
½ pint whipping cream
1 teasp. sugar
4 or 5 drops vanilla or almond extract

Line bottom and sides of ice cube tray
  with split ladyfingers.
Moisten ladyfingers with brandy but
  do not saturate.
Arrange partly thawed peach slices over
  ladyfingers.
Whip cream, adding sugar and flavoring.
Top the dessert with whipped cream.
If you wish to be extra fancy, sprinkle
  top of whipped cream with toasted
  slivered almonds.
Cover ice tray with wax paper and
  freeze for at least 6 hours.
When serving, cut across tray to form
  narrow slices. (Remove from freezer
Serves 8   20 minutes before serving.)

159

Sleeping Cookies

And you sleep, too, while They're baking!

2 egg whites
1/8 Teasp. salt
3/4 cup sugar
1 Teasp. vanilla
6 oz. chocolate chips
1 cup chopped walnuts

Preheat oven to 400°.
Chop nuts and set aside.
Beat egg whites at high speed until
    frothy — with electric beater.
Add salt, continuing to beat.
Add sugar, a bit at a time, beating
    all the while. Beat until stiff.
Add vanilla, still beating.
Fold in chips and nuts.
Grease cookie sheets well — even if
    they are Teflon. Put batter
    on sheets using heaping
    Teaspoonsful.
Put in oven. Turn it off! Go to
    bed — read a good book — just
    leave cookies alone for at
    least 3 hours.
They freeze well and thaw quickly.

160

Canton Dessert
But it's not Chinese!

4 cups apples, peeled, cored, and chopped fine
   (takes about 5 or 6 apples)

2 cups sugar
2 eggs, beaten
½ cup salad oil
2 teaspoons vanilla
2 cups flour
2 teaspoons baking soda (not powder).
2 teaspoons cinnamon
1 teaspoon salt
1 cup chopped walnuts

Mix apples with sugar and set aside while
   you do the rest.

Mix eggs and salad oil together and beat
   a bit. Add vanilla to this.

Sift together the dry ingredients.

Now add the egg mixture to apple-sugar
   and mix well.

Next add the dry ingredients, mixing well.
Fold in nuts.

Put all in greased, floured 9" x 13" flat baking
   dish and bake at 325° for 35-40 minutes.
Serve warm ~ or cool in dish. It's great plain,
   topped with whipped cream, vanilla ice
   cream, or hard sauce. Freezes well.

161

Paul's Easiest Cookies

And he grins when he even <u>Talks</u>
about These!

1 pkg. (6 oz.) butterscotch bits
3/4 cup peanut butter — smooth or chunky
4 cups Cornflakes

Put bits and peanut butter in Top of a
large double boiler. Cover and melt.
Stir vigorously occasionally so
The bits will smooth out.

When smooth, fold in Cornflakes, and
mix gently but well until all
flakes are coated.

Pour into 8" x 8" well greased flat
dish or pan. Spread around so
That it is pretty even on Top.

Cover with plastic wrap and refrigerate.
Chill about 2 hours — 'Til firm.
Cut in squares or bars. Keep
in refrigerater until serving —
so They won't get sticky.

162

Holiday Party Dessert

Ideal to keep on hand in the freezer during the holiday season!

1 quart brandied mincemeat
1/2 cup brandy
2 quarts (not 1/2 gal.) french vanilla ice cream
5 tablespoons butter, melted
2 cups crushed graham cracker crumbs
    bitter chocolate

Two days ahead remove mincemeat from
    jar and pour brandy over it. Let this
    marinate in refrigerator for 2 days.
Let ice cream soften a bit (easier to soften
    2 qts. than 1/2 gal.!)
Mix butter with crumbs and line bottom
    of flat baking dish (mine is 10" x 14".)
    Pack crumbs down. Brown in 350° oven
    for 3 minutes and cool.

Drain mincemeat.
Make a layer of ice cream on your crust—
    about 1 1/2" thick.
Top with a layer of mincemeat and then
    another layer of ice cream. This
    may come up above top of your dish.
Using large part of your grater, shave
    bitter chocolate on top.
Cover with adhering type wax paper — so
    it doesn't ice up on top — and then with
    aluminum foil.
Freeze. Serve frozen to 12-15 guests.
(I remove this from freezer about noon and put it
    in freezing compartment of refrigerator. Makes
    it easier to cut.)

163

Annapolis Angel Food Dessert

Hard on your dieting guests, but
  They'll never resist it!

2 bags chocolate bits (6 oz. each)
6 Teasp. warm water
3 eggs, separated
3 Tblsp. powdered sugar
½ cup chopped walnuts
1½ cups whipping cream
1 unfrosted angel cake (9½")

Melt chocolate bits in Top of double boiler.

Add water and stir to mix. When all is
  melted and mixed, remove from fire.

Beat egg yolks with powdered sugar and
  add To chocolate mixture slowly.

Add chopped nuts. (Don't give up! This
  is usually hard to mix!)

Beat egg whites until stiff and fold into
  above mixture.

Whip cream and fold it in.

Place frosting in refrigerator for 12 hours.

Cut angel cake horizontally into 3 layers.
  Cover each layer with frosting - reassemble
  cake - frost Top and sides and place in
  refrigerator for another 12 hours.

Serves 12

164

Topping for Vanilla Ice Cream
Do you have a pear Tree? Try This!

1 generous quart pears – washed, peeled, and
    cut into Tiny pieces
5 skimpy cups sugar
  grated rind of one fresh lemon
  juice of one fresh lemon
  juice of one fresh orange
5 whole cloves
1 Teaspoon cinnamon

Put all Together in a 3-qt. pan.
Stir well and bring To a boil. Be
    careful To Turn down heat as
    it nears The Top of The pan, or
    it will boil over.

Boil slowly, stirring often, for 30
    minutes – uncovered.

Put in clean small jars, cover and
    freeze. Thaw before using.

We have served This To many an
    appreciative guest.

165

Frozen Cheese Cake Pie

You can keep it frozen for weeks!

Graham Cracker Crust:
   1 cup graham cracker crumbs
   1/4 cup sugar
   1/2 cup finely chopped almonds
      (save some for decoration)
   1/4 cup butter, melted (more if you like)

Roll graham crackers fine. Add sugar and
   nuts (saving some) and mix with butter.
Line pie pan.

Filling:
   2 eggs
   3 pkgs. (3 oz. each) cream cheese, softened
   1/2 cup sugar
   1/2 teaspoon vanilla

Beat eggs until lemon colored and, with-
   out washing beater, beat cheese,
   sugar, and vanilla together. Add
   beaten eggs and stir until blended.
Turn into crust and bake 20 minutes
   in 325° oven.

Topping:
   2 cups commercial sour cream
   5 tablespoons granulated sugar
   1/2 teaspoon vanilla

Mix the above and spread on pie
   while it is hot and return to
   oven for 5 minutes.
Decorate around the edges with
   chopped nuts.
Freeze

166

Special Butterscotch Sauce

Lasts weeks in the refrigerator or can be frozen!

1 1/2 cups brown sugar
2/3 cup light corn syrup
1/4 cup butter
4 drops vinegar
1/3 cup cream

Combine sugar, syrup, and butter
  and slowly cook to a soft ball
  stage.
Remove from heat.
Add vinegar and stir thoroughly.
Slowly add cream, stirring constantly.

Serve hot or cold. —

167

Cookies for The Kids

And so easy That They can make Them!

1 Cup smooth peanut butter
1 egg, slightly beaten with a fork
1 cup sugar
    chocolate bits or peanuts — optional

Mix all Together and roll into balls
    The size of a walnut.

Put on slightly greased cookie sheet
    about 1½" apart. Using a fork,
    smash down each cookie about
    half way. (At This point you
    can plop a chocolate bit or a
    peanut in The center of each if
    you like.)

Bake at 350° for 10-12 minutes
    until lightly browned.

The "flour-less cookie!"

Makes about 30 —

Favorite Bars

And they freeze beautifully!

3 cups flour

2 1/2 Teaspoons baking powder

1/2 Teaspoon salt

2 1/4 cups dark brown sugar

2/3 cup butter or margarine, melted

4 eggs, beaten

1 large pkg. (12 oz.) chocolate bits

2 Teaspoons vanilla

Sift Together the flour, baking powder, and salt.

Add sugar To melted shortening, creaming well.

Add eggs, flour mixture, bits and vanilla, creaming well after each addition.

Spread in 9" x 13" greased pan or baking dish. (You must use this size!)

Bake at 350° for 25 minutes. They should come out light brown and not overcooked. Cool in pan out of oven before cutting.

Makes 50-60 bars about 1 1/4" x 1 1/4".

Quick but Tasty Desserts with no Advance Preparation

It's easy to keep the ingredients for several of these on hand ready for unexpected guests.

1. Top a chilled slice of pineapple with a scoop of pineapple ice. Make a slight indentation on top of ice and pour in 2 or 3 Tblsp. Creme de Menthe.

2. Top coffee ice cream with grated semi-sweet chocolate.

3. Top a serving of vanilla ice cream with several Tblsp. of Cointreau.

4. Top mocha ice cream with hot chocolate sauce.

5. Top lime ice with crushed chocolate bits.

6. Top a saucer of fresh raspberries with several Tblsp. commercial sour cream. Top sour cream with one half Tblsp. brown sugar.

170

My Favorite Dip

2 pkgs. cream cheese
2 beef bouillon cubes
   boiling water
   mayonnaise
5 green onions, minced
1/8 Tsp. Spice Islands Beau Monde
   Seasoning

Cream Together the cheese.
Dissolve bouillon cubes in smallest
   possible amount of water (about
   1/4 cup.) Add To cheese.
Add onion and Beau Monde.
Mix well and refrigerate.

When ready To serve, add mayonnaise and mix until dip is
   right consistency.

171

Cheese Roll

You'll love it!

1 lb. yellow cheese
2 pkgs. cream cheese (3 oz. each)
1 cup cashew nuts
2 cloves garlic, minced
   paprika

Put yellow cheese through food grinder,
   using the finest blade.
Soften and whip the cream cheese.
Put cashews through grinder - same blade.
Mix all ingredients, except paprika, well.
Shape into a roll about 1½ inches in
   diameter.
Then roll in lots of paprika. The roll
   should be really red on the outside.
Wrap in wax paper and refrigerate.
When ready to serve, slice very thin
   and place on round crackers.
This keeps well in your refrigerator
   or may be frozen.

172

Unusual Appetizer

I hope you like sprouts!

1 pkg. (10 oz.) frozen Brussels sprouts
1/2 cup juice from a bottle of dill pickles

Thaw sprouts and cook minimum
amount of time. Drain.

Put in a flat dish - I use a loaf
baking dish - and pour the
pickle juice over them. Put
in refrigerator overnight.

The next morning spoon the juice
over them again.

When ready to serve, drain, and
serve with toothpicks.

The friend who gave me this said
those who claim they dislike sprouts
eat the most!

173

Truly Delicious Dip

And it must be made 2 or 3 days ahead!

2/3 Cup commercial sour cream
2/3 Cup mayonnaise
1 Teaspoon onion salt
1/4 Teaspoon Beau Monde seasoning
1 Teaspoon dry dill weed
1 Tablespoon minced parsley (use scissors)

Combine everything well and put in
    refrigerator To mellow.

Serve with chips, raw vegetables,
    or crackers.

174

Clam Canapes

One of my most used recipes.

1 pkg. cream cheese (3 oz.)
1 can minced clams, drained
  salt to taste
  dash of red pepper
3/4 Teasp. Worcestershire Sauce
1 Teasp. minced green onion

Whip the cheese with a fork.
Add the clams and mix well.
Add remaining ingredients and
  whip well.
Place in the refrigerator in a
  covered dish.

When ready to serve, heap generously
  on plain white salty crackers and
  bake at 300° for 20 minutes.
You may sprinkle with paprika
  for "looks."

Ready Roll-Ups

These are just sitting in the freezer waiting
to rescue you when you have unexpected
company for cocktails!

1 pkg. (8 oz.) cream cheese
8 oz. bleu cheese
1 can (4½ oz.) chopped ripe olives, well
    drained
24-28 slices white bread, crusts removed
    melted butter or oleo (about 6 oz.)

Cream together the cheeses.

Add olives and mix well.

Roll each slice of bread firmly, using a rolling
    pin or a heavy glass.

Spread each slice with the mixture, being
    sure to bring it all the way to edge of
    bread.

Cut each slice of bread into 3 strips. Roll up
    each strip snugly. (if filling pops out
    at sides, remove it.)

Roll your roll-ups one by one lightly in the
    melted butter and put them on slightly
    greased cookie sheets, seam side down.
    Each should be a firm, neat, little packet.
    Place cookie sheets in freezer. when
    thoroughly frozen, remove roll-ups and
    place in plastic bags. Keep in freezer.

When ready, put as many as you need on a
    cookie sheet and bake at 350° until
    brown - about 30 minutes. Do not
    thaw first.

176

Double Cheese Dip

1 Triangle Roquefort cheese — or about
   1/3 cup Bleu cheese
2 pkgs. cream cheese (3-oz. size)
1 Tblsp. chopped fresh parsley
2 Tblsp. chopped green onions
   dash of cayenne
   dash of Worcestershire sauce
2 heaping Tblsp. mayonnaise
4 level Tblsp. commercial sour cream
1/4 Teasp. horseradish
   salt to taste

Cream cheeses together.
Add remaining ingredients — mix well —
   do not refrigerate, just set aside.
When ready, serve with potato chips.

If you place this in the refrigerator
   for several hours, it will harden and
   become an excellent dip for carrot
   sticks.

Crab Meat Spread
So good — serve on crackers!

1 pkg. (6 oz.) frozen pre-cooked King crab
    meat — or 1 can
1 can (5 oz.) water chestnuts, drained
2 Tablespoons soy sauce
½ cup real mayonnaise
2 Tablespoons minced green onions

Thaw and drain The crab meat
Chop The water chestnuts
Mix all Together and place in re-
    frigerator so flavors will blend.

Note: This does not come out
    as well if you use other Than
    King crab meat.

Roquefort Ball

How about this for a Christmas
remembrance to neighbors and nearby
friends?

1 lb. Roquefort cheese
2 pkgs. (3 oz. each) cream cheese, beaten
1 tablespoon minced green onion
1 teaspoon Worcestershire sauce
1 tablespoon paprika
2 tablespoons brandy
1 cup chopped walnuts — or more

Mix all together, except nuts, and
    roll into a ball.
Chill for at least an hour in the
    refrigerator.
Roll in walnuts.

Make several days ahead and
    keep chilled.
Serve with crackers.

Freezes well. (Thaw before serving!.)

179

Caviar Dip

1 8-oz. pkg. cream cheese
1 pint commercial sour cream
1 Tblsp. minced yellow onion
1 small jar black or red caviar.

Whip cheese and mix with sour
    cream.
Add onion.
Add caviar and mix all well.
Refrigerate.
Serve with waffle style chips
    To 12-14 guests.

Olive Roll

No one will guess what's in this —
some think it's truffles!

1 pkg. (8 oz.) cream cheese
8 oz. bleu cheese
½ cube (2 oz.) butter or margarine
2 cans (about 4 oz. each) chopped ripe olives
1 Tablespoon lemon juice
2 Tablespoons fresh minced onion
parsley, snipped finely with scissors

Cream together the cheeses and butter
until smooth.

Drain each can of olives separately into a
large strainer and press out all the
moisture with your hands. Add olives
to above — also lemon juice and onion.

Make a long roll (about 1½" in diameter) or
you may find it easier to make 2
shorter rolls. This is sort of messy,
so I do it between sheets of waxy
paper, rolling it back and forth. Chill
overnight (still in wax paper) in
refrigerator.

Before serving, roll in parsley.
Serve with crackers. It's really good! 181

Special Dip

Are you and your friends on a lo-cholesterol and lo-fat diet — but you just _must_ have a dip?

1 Cup lo-fat cottage cheese
½ Cup Tomato ketchup
1 Tablespoon Imitation Mayonnaise
2 Tablespoons French dressing
2 Tablespoons buttermilk
½ Teaspoon horseradish sauce
1 green onion, minced
¼ Teaspoon salt substitute
⅛ Teaspoon coarse ground pepper

Put everything in blender and mix until smooth.
Make a day ahead, and keep covered in refrigerator.

Serve with sticks or slices of fresh vegetables. (Sometime try peeled and sliced kohlrabi.)

182

Fun Finger Rolls

1 pkg. (7.5-oz. Tube-like pkg.) refrigerator
Buttermilk Biscuits

⅛ lb. butter or margarine

Poppy seeds or sesame seeds or grated
Parmesan cheese or mixed herbs, etc.

Melt butter in 7½" x 12" flat baking dish
in oven.

Meanwhile divide each of the 10 biscuits in
half and roll into finger size.

Roll each in whichever seasoning you
prefer — or do several — or make
up some of your own!

When butter is melted, roll it around in
the dish so it covers the bottom.

Now put your rolls in the butter with
sides not touching.

Bake at 400° for 10 to 12 minutes or until
golden brown. Serve immediately or
cool, put in plastic bag gently, and
reheat later in pan covered with
foil (not the plastic bag!) at 350°
for 5 to 8 minutes or until hot through.

Makes 20 little loaf-like rolls.

183

Bran Muffins

This batter keeps well in the refrigerator!.

1/2 cup shortening (like Crisco)
1 1/2 cup sugar
2 eggs
1 cup boiling water
2 cups All Bran cereal
2 1/2 cups flour
2 Teasp. baking soda
1 Teasp. salt
1 cup 100% Bran cereal
2 cups buttermilk
   raisins (optional)

Cream shortening and sugar together.
Add eggs and mix well.
Pour boiling water over All Bran.
Sift together the flour, soda, and salt.
Add Bran-water to shortening-sugar-eggs
   and mix well.
Stir in the 100% All Bran.

(cont'd)   184

Bran Muffins

(continued from preceding page)

Add flour mixture and mix gently but well.

Fold in buttermilk and mix just until all is thoroughly moistened.

Add raisins if desired.

Fill greased muffin tins 2/3 full and bake at 375° for 15 to 17 minutes.

Keep batter in refrigerator.

Makes almost 2 quarts of batter.

Fun to make in mid-December and serve "fresh baked" to your Christmas houseguests for breakfast!

Filled French Rolls

Fun To make-and fun To eat!

8 French rolls
1/2 cup softened margarine - not melted
1/2 cup grated Parmesan cheese
2 Tblsp. salad oil
1/2 cup finely chopped fresh parsley
1 clove garlic, finely chopped
1/2 Teasp. sweet basil
    salt To Taste

Turn each roll on its side and cut into
    1/2 inch slices - but do not cut all The
    way Through The roll.
Make The filling by blending The margarine
    with The remaining ingredients.
Spread The filling beTween each slice.
Wrap each roll individually in aluminum
    foil. Set aside until needed.

Bake in a 375° oven for 20 minutes.
 Serve in The foil. Each person Keeps his
    roll hot by rewrapping in The foil.
    Wonderful for a barbecue in your
    patio!
Rolls may be frozen in Their foil wrappers.
    If not Thawed, bake 10 minutes longer.

186

Marinade for Beef

And, in particular, This is absolutely
marvelous for London Broil!

½ cup salad oil
½ cup soy sauce
½ cup red wine
1 Tablespoon lemon juice
2 cloves garlic, finely minced
¼ Teaspoon pepper
¼ Teaspoon salt
1 Teaspoon monosodium glutamate (MSG)
1 Tablespoon sugar

Mix all Together and beat with egg beater.
Marinate meat overnight, Turning
occasionally — in refrigerator.

Marinade for Fish

Makes even a "so-so" fish taste great!

1 clove garlic, finely minced
½ cup soy sauce
½ cup red wine
    juice of half a large lemon
    minced green onion (see below)

Make 2 or 3 slant-wise gashes in
    each side of fish.
Marinate several hours, turning once.
Sprinkle with green onion before
    baking but not before broiling or
    onion will burn.

This marinade is the right amount
    for 2 fish the size of an average
    rockfish. Use a flat-ish dish.

Christmas Breakfast

You make it The day before, and it bakes
happily while you open your gifts Xmas
morning!

7 slices white bread (regular, not thin sliced)
2 pkgs. (4 oz. each) shredded cheddar cheese
6 eggs
3 cups milk
1/2 Teaspoon salt
1/4 Teaspoon pepper
1 Teaspoon dry mustard
3 strips bacon, cut in half

Trim crusts from bread. Crumble bread.
Mix bread and cheese and spread in bottom
    of greased 7 1/2" x 12" flat baking dish.
Beat eggs and milk together and stir in
    The salt, pepper, and mustard. Pour
    This over bread-cheese.
Lay bacon on Top.
Refrigerate overnight.
The next morning bake, uncovered, at
    350° for 50 to 55 minutes.

Remove from oven just after guests sit down.
Otherwise, it may tend to sink — tastes just as
great — but doesn't look as glamorous.

Serves 6 —

189

Coffee Strudel

Great for Tea or a coffee!

2 cups flour
1/2 lb. butter
1 cup sour cream
  apricot or cherry jam
  raisins or currants
  chopped walnuts
  sugar
  cinnamon
  powdered sugar

Knead together the flour, butter, and
  sour cream. Refrigerate over night.
The next day separate into 3 or 4
  parts. Roll out thin and spread
  with a thin layer of each of
  the remaining ingredients, except
  the powdered sugar.
Roll up and place on a greased
  cookie sheet.
Bake at 350° until crust turns
  golden brown — about 20 to 30
  minutes.
Remove from oven and let cool a
  few minutes
Cut diagonally into one inch
  pieces and sprinkle with
  powdered sugar.

190

Special Tea

A favorite with the college group!

1 large (18 oz.) jar TANG
½ cup instant Tea
1 ½ cups sugar
1 Teasp. ground cinnamon
½ Teasp. ground cloves
    lemon slices

Mix Together all but lemon and
    keep in closed jar.
For each cup of boiling water,
    use 2 or 3 heaping Teaspoons
    of mixture.
Add a Thin slice of lemon To
    each cup of hot Tea.

Simple Sauces

① For asparagus, broccoli, or potatoes —

1 jar CHEESE WHIZ
  same amount of mushroom soup,
    undiluted
Mix together and heat thoroughly
  in top of double boiler. Difficult?

② For Spareribs
1 can (15 3/4 oz.) pineapple chunks
  and juice
2 tablespoons soy sauce
1/2 cup brown sugar
1/2 cup ketchup
2 teaspoons powdered ginger
Mix all together.

1 place about 4 lbs. spareribs on a
rack in baking pan. Sprinkle with
salt and pepper. Bake at 400° for
45 minutes. Pour off grease and
remove rack. Put ribs in pan
and pour sauce over them. Bake
1/2 hour more, basting occasionally,
with oven turned down to 300°.
Serves 4 —

Cold Sauce for Ham

2 cucumbers - peel and remove seeds
1 cup real mayonnaise
5 Teasp. prepared horseradish
4 Teasp. wet mustard
1 Teasp. salt
   dash of red pepper

Chop cucumbers. There should be about
   1 2/3 cups.

Mix well with remaining ingredients.
Serve chilled.

Hot Sauce for Ham

1 glass currant or boysenberry jelly.
   rind (grated) and juice of 1 orange
1/4 Teasp. nutmeg
1/4 Teasp. cinnamon
1/8 Teasp. powdered ginger
1 jigger port wine

Combine all except port.

When ready, place in top of double
   boiler until hot.
Add port just before you take it
   off the heat. Stir all gently.

193

Peach Flip

You'll like your peaches like this!

1 pkg. (10 oz.) frozen peaches
1 can (6 oz.) frozen lemonade
1 lemonade can Vodka

Thaw peaches and lemonade enough
   to be manageable.
Pour all in blender. Fill blender to
   top with ice.

My husband says:

   "Whip — Sip — Flip!"

(If your blender can't cope with many ice
cubes, crush ice first. Or just add a couple
of cubes at a time — will be slushy.)

194

San Francisco Cocktail

Before a festive luncheon it is often fun to serve an unusual cocktail. Try This!

2 Fifths of White Port
8 oz. light Rum
juice of 4 lemons
Maraschino cherries - or fresh strawberries

Chill the Port
Add the Rum and lemon juice
Mix well, place in a glass container and refrigerate.

When ready to serve, place a cherry or fresh strawberry in each glass, stir the cocktail well, and serve very cold in wine or martini glasses. You may add a little ice to the shaker to keep it cold.

Serves 12-16

Ready Breakfast
Really provides variety!

When ground round is specially priced, buy several pounds and make into patties.

Cover a cookie sheet with foil and put patties - almost touching - on sheet. Put in freezer.

When thoroughly frozen, remove patties from cookie sheet and put in plastic bag. Return to freezer.

You can fry these frozen (takes a little longer) or take desired number from freezer and put in refrigerator the night before you want to use them.

Great for breakfast — and the kids do love a handy hamburger for lunch or after school.

You can do the same with pork sausage from your butcher - not previously frozen.

Buy slices of cooked ham, cut in serving sizes and follow same method. Also steak.

196

Ideas

Surround your Christmas Turkey with this:
  Place canned peach halves in baking dish.
  Fill centers with mincemeat.
  Cover bottom of dish with peach juice.
  Place in 300° oven until hot.

Green Beans
  Boil 2 pkgs. green beans 7 minutes.
    Drain and place in 1½ qt. casserole.
  Mix 1 can undiluted mushroom soup
    with ¼ soup can milk. Pour over beans.
  Just before baking, fold in 1 can French
    fried onions, saving some for top.
  Bake, uncovered, at 300° for 35 minutes.

Green Salad
  Crumble 1 wedge (1¼ oz.) roquefort cheese
    into 1 small carton sour cream.
  Mash cheese and stir until fairly smooth.
  Add 1 heaping Tblsp. mayonnaise, juice of
    ½ a lemon, 1 green onion (minced), and
    at least ⅛ teasp. black pepper - freshly
    ground if possible.
  Refrigerate, covered.
  Just before adding dressing to salad,
    add 2 small cans chilled, drained,
    seedless grapes to salad greens.
  Toss all and serve.

Conversion Tables
Approximate — but close enough!

Liquid Measures

American	Metric
1 Teaspoon	5 milliliters
1 Tablespoon	15 "
1 cup (8 oz.)	237 "
1 pint (16 oz.)	473 "
1 Quart (32 oz.)	946 "

Solid Measures

1 oz.	28 grams
1 lb.	454 "

Oven Temperatures

Fahrenheit	Celsius or Centigrade
250° - 275°	121° - 135°
275° - 325°	135° - 163°
350° - 375°	177° - 190°
400° - 450°	204° - 230°
450° - 500°	230° - 260°

"Make It Now" recipes are based on
American (and Fahrenheit)
measures.

198

Index

Main Dishes

With Beef (cont'd)

With Lamb

cont'd

Main Dishes
With Chicken (or Turkey)

201

Main Dishes (Cont'd)

With Pork

With Eggs

Cont'd

Main Dishes

With Seafood

Cont'd

203

Main Dishes

(cont'd)

Cont'd.

Side Dishes and Vegetables

Soups

Salads

Cont'd

Salads (Cont'd)

Salad Dressings

Cont'd

207

Cont'd

Desserts (cont'd)

Desserts

Cookies (Cont'd)

Rolls, Etc.

Appetizers

Cont'd

210

Cont'd

One half of the author's profit
from all of the "Make
It Now" books is given to:

The Cystic Fibrosis Foundation
6000 Executive Blvd.
Suite 309
Rockville, Md. 20852

For further information, write to:
Barbara Goodfellow
409 First Street
Coronado, Calif. 92118

213

Notes

Notes

Notes